## CGP helps you know your stuff!

Want to learn all the essential grammar and vocabulary for AQA GCSE Spanish? This CGP Knowledge Organiser is here to help!

We've condensed every topic down to the key words, phrases and explanations, making it all easy to memorise.

There's also a matching Knowledge Retriever book that'll test you on every page — perfect for making sure you know it all!

## CGP — still the best! ☺

Our sole aim here at CGP is to produce the highest quality books — carefully written, immaculately presented and dangerously close to being funny.

Then we work our socks off to get them out to you — at the cheapest possible prices.

# Contents

## Topic 11 — Grammar




Published by CGP.

Editors: Siân Butler, Gabrielle Richardson, Hannah Roscoe.
Contributor: Jacqui Richards

With thanks to Becca Lakin and Encarna Aparicio-Dominguez for the proofreading.
With thanks to Lottie Edwards for the copyright research.

ISBN: 978 1 78908 718 5

Printed by Elanders Ltd, Newcastle upon Tyne.
Clipart from Corel®

Based on the classic CGP style created by Richard Parsons

# Numbers

## Los números

| TICKET # | TICKET # | TICKET # | TICKET # |
|---|---|---|---|
| 14 | 29 | 73 | 130 |
| catorce | veintinueve | setenta y tres | ciento treinta |

| TICKET # | TICKET # | TICKET # | TICKET # |
|---|---|---|---|
| 450 | 1942 | 2010 | 3816 |
| cuatrocientos cincuenta | mil novecientos cuarenta y dos | dos mil diez | tres mil ochocientos dieciséis |

Es la segunda vez que he jugado a la lotería.
**It's the second time that I've entered the lottery.**

Para mí, es la sexta. Ya he ganado un par de premios pequeños.
**For me, it's the sixth. I've already won a couple of small prizes.**

Me encantaría ganar el primer premio. ¡Es dos millones de euros!
**I would love to win the first prize. It's two million euros!**

Preferiría el tercero o el cuarto. Ambos son coches de lujo.
**I would prefer the third or fourth. They are both luxury cars.**

## Number phrases

| | |
|---|---|
| una docena | ***a dozen*** |
| unos/as | ***some / a few / about*** |
| numeroso/a | ***numerous*** |
| varios/as | ***several*** |
| ambos/as | ***both*** |
| añadir | ***to add*** |
| el/la máximo/a | ***maximum*** |
| el/la mínimo/a | ***minimum*** |
| por ciento | ***percent*** |
| una cifra | ***figure (e.g. 1)*** |

# Times and Dates

## ¿Qué hora es?

Son las seis y cuarto. El partido termina a las siete menos cuarto.
**It's quarter past six. The match finishes at quarter to seven.**

Empieza a la una así que debemos partir a las once y media.
**It starts at one o'clock so we must set off at half past eleven.**

**Many Spanish-speaking countries also use the** 24-hour clock.

Son las veintiuna horas treinta minutos. **It's 21:30.**

Son las tres horas catorce minutos. **It's 03:14.**

Son las diecinueve horas cincuenta y cinco minutos. **It's 19:55.**

## Useful time phrases

| | |
|---|---|
| Tengo un examen pasado mañana. | I have an exam the day after tomorrow. |
| Está en oferta durante quince días. | It's on offer for a fortnight. |
| Voy al gimnasio cada tres días. | I go to the gym every three days. |
| Anoche, fui al teatro en el centro. | Last night, I went to the theatre in the town centre. |
| Esta tarde, voy de compras con mi hermanastro. | This afternoon, I'm going shopping with my stepbrother. |
| El año pasado, viajé a Polonia para visitar a mis abuelos. | Last year, I travelled to Poland to visit my grandparents. |
| Nos conocimos anteayer. | We met the day before yesterday. |
| Tenemos que ir al mercado mañana por la mañana. | We have to go to the market tomorrow morning. |

# Times and Dates

## Los días de la semana

| | |
|---|---|
| lunes | *Monday* |
| martes | *Tuesday* |
| miércoles | *Wednesday* |
| jueves | *Thursday* |
| viernes | *Friday* |
| sábado | *Saturday* |
| domingo | *Sunday* |

El fin de semana, cogimos el tren a Buñol.
**At the weekend, we took the train to Buñol.**

Los miércoles, voy al cine con mis amigos.
**On Wednesdays, I go to the cinema with my friends.**

## Los meses del año

| | | | | | |
|---|---|---|---|---|---|
| enero | *January* | mayo | *May* | septiembre | *September* |
| febrero | *February* | junio | *June* | octubre | *October* |
| marzo | *March* | julio | *July* | noviembre | *November* |
| abril | *April* | agosto | *August* | diciembre | *December* |

| | |
|---|---|
| En invierno, iremos a esquiar. | In winter, we will go skiing. |
| La primavera es mi estación preferida. | Spring is my favourite season. |
| Cada verano, me gusta montar a caballo. | Every summer, I like to go horse riding. |
| A mis padres y a mí nos encanta ir de pesca en otoño. | My parents and I love to go fishing in autumn. |

## ¿Qué fecha es?

**In Spanish, you say 'the three of May' not 'the third of May'. This applies to all dates apart from 'the first', which uses 'el primero de' or 'el uno de'.**

el tres de mayo
**(on) the third of May**

Es el primero de / el uno de febrero.
**It's the first of February.**

# Questions

## Asking questions

**Put question marks at the beginning and end of a statement to make it a question.**

¿Tu corbata es azul? **Is your tie blue?**  **Raise your voice at the end to show it's a question.**

**Remember that question words need accents.**

¿Cómo se dice 'cake' en español? **How do you say 'cake' in Spanish?**

¿Cuándo es tu cumpleaños? **When is your birthday?**

¿Por qué haces eso? **Why are you doing that?**

¿Cuántos/as tienes? **How many do you have?**

¿De dónde eres? **Where are you from?**

¿Quién va? **Who is going?**

¿Cuánto es? **How much is it?**  **If 'cuánto' is followed by a noun, it needs to agree, e.g. ¿Cuánta agua bebes al día?**

## Tengo una pregunta

| | |
|---|---|
| ¿Qué día es hoy? | What day is it today? |
| ¿Cuántos años tiene tu primo? | How old is your cousin? |
| ¿A qué hora empieza? | At what time does it start? |
| ¿Por cuánto tiempo has estado aquí? | How long have you been here? |
| ¿Cuál es tu fruta favorita? | What is your favourite fruit? |
| ¿De qué color era el abrigo? | What colour was the coat? |
| ¿Cuánto vale este cuadro de Picasso? | How much is this painting by Picasso worth? |

# Being Polite

## Los saludos

| | | | |
|---|---|---|---|
| buenos días | *good day / good morning* | hasta luego | *see you later* |
| buenas tardes | *good afternoon / good evening* | hasta el lunes | *see you on Monday* |
| buenas noches | *good night* | hasta mañana | *see you tomorrow* |
| | | hasta pronto | *see you soon* |

¿Qué tal? / ¿Cómo estás?
**How are you? (informal)**

¿Cómo está?
**How are you? (formal)**

(no) muy bien
**(not) very well**

así así
**so-so**

fatal
**terrible**

## Por favor y gracias

| | | | |
|---|---|---|---|
| muchas gracias | *thank you very much* | por favor | *please* |
| Eres muy amable. | *That's very kind of you. (informal)* | De nada. | *You're welcome.* |
| Es muy amable. | *That's very kind of you. (formal)* | Lo siento mucho. | *I'm really sorry.* |
| | | vale | *OK* |
| | | ¡Claro! | *Of course!* |

¡Por favor! / ¡Perdone!
**Excuse me! (E.g. for asking someone the way)**

¡Con permiso!
**Excuse me! (E.g. for wanting to get past someone)**

## Le presento a...

Le presento a Ana.
**May I introduce Ana?**

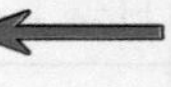

**Use 'Te presento a...' with someone you call 'tú'.**

Este es Arturo.
**This is Arturo.**

**Use 'Esta es...' for introducing someone female.**

Encantado.
**Pleased to meet you.**

**Use 'Encantada' if you're female. You can also say 'mucho gusto', which stays the same for both genders.**

# Being Polite

## Asking for things politely

Use 'quisiera' ('I would like') to ask for something politely.

Quisiera un café.
I would like a coffee.

Quisiera hablar.
I would like to talk.

You can also use the verb 'poder' ('to be able to').

¿Puedo sentarme?
May I sit down?

¿Puedo ir al baño?
May I go to the toilet?

## Tú y usted

There are four different ways to say 'you' in Spanish.

1. 'Tú' — for one person who's your friend, a family member or of a similar age.

   ¿Dónde estás?
   Where are you?

   ¿Qué opinas?
   What do you think?

2. 'Vosotros/as' — for a group of two or more people that you know. Only use 'vosotras' if the whole group is female.

   ¿Dónde estáis?
   Where are you?

   ¿Qué opináis?
   What do you think?

3. 'Usted' — for one person who's older than you or someone you don't know. It uses the 'he/she/it' part of the verb.

   ¿Dónde está?
   Where are you?

   ¿Qué opina?
   What do you think?

4. 'Ustedes' — for a group of two or more people that you don't know. It uses the 'they' part of the verb.

   ¿Dónde están?
   Where are you?

   ¿Qué opinan?
   What do you think?

# Opinions

## ¿Qué piensas de..?

¿Qué piensas de mi bolso?
**What do you think of my bag?**

¿Lo encuentras entretenido?
**Do you find it entertaining?**

¿Cuál es tu opinión de esta canción? **What is your opinion of this song?**

| | |
|---|---|
| El deporte me aburre. No creo que sea emocionante. | Sport bores me. I don't think it's exciting. |
| Me parece divertido y me hace reír. | I think it's fun and it makes me laugh. |
| Es verdad. Las telenovelas no me gustan nada. | It's true. I don't like soap operas at all. |
| No estoy de acuerdo. Pienso que esta novela es genial. | I don't agree. I think this novel is brilliant. |
| Me encantan las películas de aventura porque son maravillosas. | I love adventure films because they're wonderful. |
| Me interesan los documentales. | Documentaries interest me. |
| Encuentro el pescado desagradable. | I find fish unpleasant. |
| Odio la fruta. Prefiero las verduras. | I hate fruit. I prefer vegetables. |

## Creo que es...

| | | | |
|---|---|---|---|
| estupendo/a | ***fantastic*** | precioso/a | ***beautiful*** |
| fenomenal | ***great*** | increíble | ***incredible*** |
| guay | ***cool*** | interesante | ***interesting*** |
| perfecto/a | ***perfect*** | horrible | ***awful*** |
| impresionante | ***impressive*** | aburrido/a | ***boring*** |
| agradable | ***nice, kind*** | raro/a | ***strange*** |
| fabuloso/a | ***fabulous*** | ridículo/a | ***ridiculous*** |
| bonito/a | ***pretty*** | decepcionante | ***disappointing*** |

# About Yourself and Your Family

## Preséntate

Mi nombre es Gustavo. Mi apellido es Jiménez.
Tengo quince años y mi cumpleaños es el 6 de mayo.
**My name is Gustavo. My surname is Jiménez.**
**I'm 15 years old and my birthday is 6th May.**

¡Hola! Me llamo Samira. Mi fecha de nacimiento es el 19 de junio de 2006. Cumpliré quince años la semana que viene, así que somos de la misma edad.
**Hello! I'm called Samira. My date of birth is 19th June 2006. I'll turn 15 next week, so we're the same age.**

Nací en México, pero ahora soy de nacionalidad española.
**I was born in Mexico but now I'm of Spanish nationality.**

Soy de Vigo. Mis padres se mudaron de Marruecos antes de que yo naciera.
**I'm from Vigo. My parents moved from Morocco before I was born.**

## Háblame de tu familia

| | | | |
|---|---|---|---|
| el padre | ***father*** | el hermanastro | ***stepbrother*** |
| la madre | ***mother*** | la hermanastra | ***stepsister*** |
| los padres | ***parents*** | el/la hijo/a único/a | ***only child*** |
| el hermano | ***brother*** | el/la gemelo/a | ***twin*** |
| la hermana | ***sister*** | el marido / el esposo | ***husband*** |
| el padrastro | ***stepfather*** | la mujer / la esposa | ***wife*** |
| la madrastra | ***stepmother*** | el sobrino | ***nephew*** |

| | |
|---|---|
| Tengo muchos parientes. | I have lots of relatives. |
| Mis abuelos tienen seis hijos y veintiún nietos. | My grandparents have six children and twenty-one grandchildren. |
| En total, tengo ocho tíos, diez tías y veinte primos menores. | In total, I have eight uncles, ten aunts and twenty younger cousins. |
| También tengo una sobrina joven. | I also have a young niece. |

# Describing People

## El aspecto físico

Mi abuelo es calvo y bastante gordo. Es viejo y lleva gafas.
**My grandfather is bald and quite fat. He's old and wears glasses.**

Mi madre tiene el pelo moreno y rizado.
**My mother has dark, curly hair.**

Mi prima es altísima. Tiene los ojos marrones y el pelo negro y largo. Lleva maquillaje.
**My cousin is really tall. She has brown eyes and long, black hair. She wears make-up.**

Soy de altura mediana. Soy delgado y no tengo pecas. Soy ciego de un ojo.
**I am medium height. I'm slim and I don't have freckles. I'm blind in one eye.**

Mi hermano tiene el pelo castaño. Es guapo y no tiene barba.
**My brother has chestnut-brown hair. He's good-looking and he doesn't have a beard.**

Mi padre tiene el pelo corto y un bigote. Es sordo del oído izquierdo.
**My father has short hair and a moustache. He is deaf in his left ear.**

Mi primo es pelirrojo. Es bajo y tiene los ojos verdes.
**My cousin is red-haired. He's short and he has green eyes.**

Mi hermana tiene el pelo liso y rubio y los ojos azules. Utiliza una silla de ruedas.
**My sister has straight, blonde hair and blue eyes. She uses a wheelchair.**

# Personalities

## Mi personalidad

| | | | |
|---|---|---|---|
| animado/a | ***lively*** | sensible | ***sensitive*** |
| alegre | ***happy*** | callado/a | ***quiet*** |
| cariñoso/a | ***affectionate*** | valiente | ***brave*** |
| comprensivo/a | ***understanding*** | egoísta | ***selfish*** |
| cortés | ***polite*** | maleducado/a | ***rude*** |
| gracioso/a | ***funny*** | perezoso/a | ***lazy*** |
| hablador(a) | ***chatty / talkative*** | travieso/a | ***naughty*** |
| atrevido/a | ***daring / cheeky*** | torpe | ***clumsy*** |
| serio/a | ***serious*** | celoso/a | ***jealous*** |

## Describir personas

Mis padres son comprensivos y amables. Mi madre es habladora pero mi padre es más callado y serio.
**My parents are understanding and kind. My mother is chatty but my father is quieter and more serious.**

Mi hermana es muy atrevida y mi hermano es bastante torpe.
**My sister is very daring and my brother is quite clumsy.**

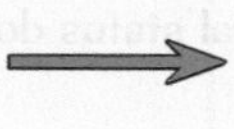

Me gustaría ser más valiente y aventurero como mi hermana.
**I'd like to be braver and more adventurous like my sister.**

Mis profesoras son simpáticas pero estrictas al mismo tiempo.
**My teachers are nice but strict at the same time.**

| | |
|---|---|
| Mi mejor amiga es siempre alegre. | My best friend is always happy. |
| Tiene un buen sentido del humor y es sensible. | She has a good sense of humour and she's sensitive. |
| Sin embargo, a veces es un poco maleducada... ...porque llega tarde cuando vamos al cine. | However, sometimes she's a bit rude... ...because she arrives late when we go to the cinema. |
| Lo encuentro muy frustrante. | I find it very frustrating. |

# Relationships and Partnership

## Las relaciones

| | |
|---|---|
| Me llevo mal con mis padres... ...debido a la barrera generacional. | I don't get on well with my parents... ...due to the generation gap. |
| No aguanto a mi hermano y nos peleamos mucho. | I can't stand my brother and we fight a lot. |
| Mi hermana me fastidia. | My sister annoys me. |
| A menudo me relaciono con mi tía. | I am often in contact with my aunt. |
| Conozco muy bien a mi novia... ...y confío en ella. | I know my girlfriend really well... ...and I trust her. |
| Fue amor a primera vista... ...y tenemos pocas disputas. | It was love at first sight... ...and we have few arguments. |

## En el futuro...

Estoy contenta de ser soltera y el estado civil no me importa demasiado.
**I am happy being single and marital status doesn't matter too much to me.**

A mi modo de ver, no es necesario casarse antes de tener hijos, pero me gustaría hacerlo de todos modos.
**The way I see it, it's not necessary to get married before having children, but I'd like to do it anyway.**

Quiero comprometerme porque estoy enamorado de mi novio. Desde mi punto de vista, las bodas son muy románticas.
**I want to get engaged because I'm in love with my boyfriend. From my point of view, weddings are very romantic.**

Debo admitir que los casamientos y los anillos me parecen demasiado caros.
**I must admit that weddings and rings seem far too expensive to me.**

En mi opinión, el matrimonio te da estabilidad.
**In my opinion, marriage gives you stability.**

Cuando tenga suficiente dinero, preferiría comprar una casa con mi pareja.
**When I have enough money, I'd prefer to buy a house with my partner.**

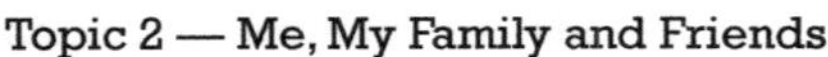

# Music

## La música

| ¿Tocas algún instrumento? | Do you play an instrument? |
|---|---|
| Toco la guitarra en un grupo de rock. | I play the guitar in a rock band. |
| Cuando era pequeño, tocaba el piano y el violín. | When I was little, I used to play the piano and the violin. |
| Canto música clásica en un coro... ...y quiero ser cantante. | I sing classical music in a choir... ...and I want to be a singer. |
| Quiero aprender a tocar la batería... ...pero mi padre no me dejará. | I want to learn to play the drums... ...but my father won't let me. |
| Mi hermana es música y toca el clarinete en una orquesta. | My sister is a musician and she plays the clarinet in an orchestra. |

## ¿Te gusta escuchar música?

Me encanta escuchar la música rap porque me hace sentir relajado.
**I love listening to rap music because it makes me feel relaxed.**

Escucho muchas grabaciones de audio de cantantes pop.
**I listen to lots of audio recordings of pop singers.**

Diría que mi género de música preferido es el hip-hop.
**I'd say that my favourite genre of music is hip-hop.**

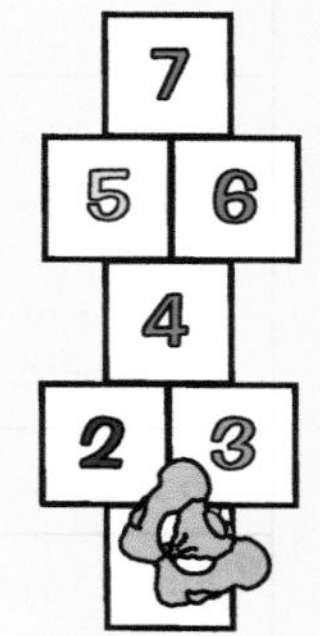


Puedo llevar la música conmigo y escucharla cuando salgo a correr, lo que me parece fenomenal.
**I can take my music with me and listen to it while I'm jogging, which seems great to me.**

Me encanta la música en directo e intento ir a muchos conciertos.
**I love live music and I try to go to lots of concerts.**

Sus videos musicales son originales y su letra es interesante.
**Their music videos are original and their lyrics are interesting.**

# Cinema and TV

## En el cine

Me gusta ir al cine con mis amigos porque las entradas son baratas.
**I like going to the cinema with my friends because the tickets are cheap.**

Es interesante ver a los actores y las actrices en sus nuevos papeles.
**It's interesting to see the actors and actresses in their new roles.**

No me gustan las películas policíacas o de ciencia ficción porque es difícil seguir la trama.
**I don't like detective or science fiction films because it's difficult to follow the plot.**

La película de acción trataba de un espía. Los efectos especiales y la banda sonora eran fenomenales.
**The action film was about a spy. The special effects and the soundtrack were great.**

Tengo ganas de ver la nueva película de terror porque el reparto está lleno de estrellas.
**I'm looking forward to seeing the new horror film because the cast is full of stars.**

## ¿Te gusta ver la tele?

| | |
|---|---|
| Me gusta ver la tele los sábados. | I like watching TV on Saturdays. |
| Mi cadena preferida es BBC1... ...porque no hay anuncios. | My favourite channel is BBC1... ...because there aren't any adverts. |
| Mucha gente se queja que las telenovelas son aburridas... ...pero no estoy de acuerdo porque me ayudan a relajarme. | Many people complain that soap operas are boring... ...but I don't agree because they help me to relax. |
| No me gusta ver las noticias. | I don't like watching the news. |
| Quisiera ver más documentales... ...y menos dibujos animados. | I'd like to see more documentaries... ...and fewer cartoons. |
| Veo los concursos con mi abuela y participamos juntos. | I watch game shows with my grandma and we join in together. |

# Food

## Las frutas

| | |
|---|---|
| la manzana | ***apple*** |
| el melocotón | ***peach*** |
| la fresa | ***strawberry*** |
| la naranja | ***orange*** |
| el plátano | ***banana*** |
| la pera | ***pear*** |
| las uvas | ***grapes*** |
| la piña | ***pineapple*** |

## Las verduras

| | |
|---|---|
| las legumbres | ***vegetables, pulses*** |
| las judías verdes | ***string beans*** |
| los champiñones | ***mushrooms*** |
| los guisantes | ***peas*** |
| la zanahoria | ***carrot*** |
| la col | ***cabbage*** |
| la cebolla | ***onion*** |
| la lechuga | ***lettuce*** |

## Otros alimentos

| | | | |
|---|---|---|---|
| la carne de vaca | ***beef*** | el gazpacho | ***cold soup*** |
| la carne de cordero | ***lamb*** | las tapas | ***bar snacks*** |
| la carne de cerdo | ***pork*** | los churros | ***long doughnuts*** |
| la carne de ternera | ***veal*** | el caramelo | ***boiled sweet*** |
| el pollo | ***chicken*** | el huevo | ***egg*** |
| la salchicha | ***sausage*** | la nata | ***cream*** |
| el chorizo | ***Spanish sausage*** | el aceite | ***oil*** |
| el pescado | ***fish*** | el té | ***tea*** |
| el arroz | ***rice*** | el zumo | ***juice*** |
| una barra de pan | ***a loaf of bread*** | la leche | ***milk*** |

## ¿Qué te gusta comer?

Para el desayuno, tomo dos tostadas con mantequilla y mermelada.
**For breakfast, I have two slices of toast with butter and jam.**

Almuerzo a la una. Suelo comer un bocadillo de jamón y queso.
**I have lunch at one o'clock. I usually eat a ham and cheese sandwich.**

Me tomo un café con galletas como merienda.
**I have a coffee with biscuits as an afternoon snack.**

Ceno un filete poco hecho con patatas hervidas y ajo asado.
**I have a rare steak with boiled potatoes and roasted garlic for dinner.**

# Eating Out

## ¡Vamos al restaurante!

| | | | |
|---|---|---|---|
| el camarero | *waiter* | tener sed | *to be thirsty* |
| la camarera | *waitress* | tener hambre | *to be hungry* |
| la carta | *menu* | la sal | *salt* |
| el tenedor | *fork* | la pimienta | *pepper* |
| el cuchillo | *knife* | el vaso | *glass* |
| la cuchara | *spoon* | la bebida | *drink* |
| el primer plato | *starter* | la cuenta | *bill* |
| el segundo plato | *main course* | la propina | *tip* |
| el plato (combinado) | *(set) dish* | incluido/a | *included* |

**Me encanta probar nueva comida, por ejemplo la china o la tailandesa.**
**I love trying new food, for example Chinese or Thai.**

**A veces ceno en restaurantes mediterráneos porque me gustan los mariscos, especialmente las gambas a la plancha o los calamares fritos.**
**Sometimes I have dinner in Mediterranean restaurants because I like seafood, especially grilled prawns or fried squid.**

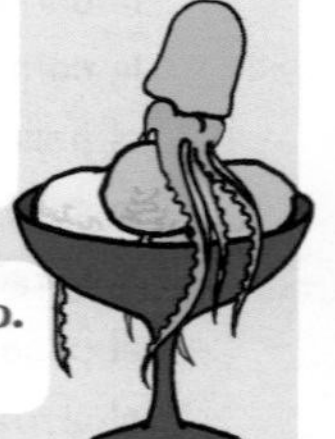

**Después de una comida grande, siempre pido algo dulce como un helado.**
**After a big meal, I always order something sweet like an ice cream.**

## ¿Qué le gustaría tomar?

| | |
|---|---|
| Quisiera una pizza picante. | I would like a spicy pizza. |
| Me gustaría la tortilla de champiñones y una ensalada. | I would like the mushroom omelette and a salad. |
| Para el postre, me apetece un pastel. | For dessert, I fancy a cake. |
| Mis abuelos quieren una copa de vino y una cerveza. | My grandparents want a glass of wine and a beer. |
| Este plato no es lo que pedí. ¿Me puede traer el correcto? | This dish isn't what I ordered. Can you bring me the right one? |

# Sport

## ¿Practicas algún deporte?

| | | | |
|---|---|---|---|
| la equitación | ***horse riding*** | los deportes de riesgo | ***adventure sports*** |
| la natación | ***swimming*** | la piscina | ***swimming pool*** |
| la vela | ***sailing*** | la pista | ***track, court, slope*** |
| la pesca | ***fishing*** | la pista de hielo | ***ice rink*** |
| el atletismo | ***athletics*** | bailar | ***to dance*** |
| el alpinismo | ***mountain climbing*** | nadar | ***to swim*** |
| el patinaje | ***skating*** | patinar | ***to skate*** |

## Mi deporte preferido es...

| | |
|---|---|
| Me gusta montar en bici... ...porque me da la oportunidad de explorar mi pueblo. | I like riding my bike... ...because it gives me the chance to explore my town. |
| Corro tres veces por semana... ...y participo en carreras de 10 km. | I run three times a week... ...and I take part in 10 km races. |
| Me encanta montar a caballo varias veces por semana. | I love going horse riding several times a week. |
| Me gusta jugar al bádminton... ...porque puedo divertirme... ...y hacer deporte a la vez. | I like playing badminton... ...because I can have fun... ...and do sport at the same time. |
| El polideportivo donde practicamos está cerca de mi casa. | The sports centre where we practise is near my house. |
| No soy exactamente deportista... ...pero el ejercicio me importa... ...ya que mejora mi salud mental. | I'm not exactly sporty... ...but exercise is important to me... ...as it improves my mental health. |
| Voy al colegio en monopatín y a veces pesco con mi padre... ...pero prefiero cocinar o leer en mi tiempo libre. | I go to school by skateboard and sometimes I fish with my father... ...but I prefer to cook or read in my free time. |

# Sport

## El deporte en directo

| | |
|---|---|
| Me encantaría visitar un estadio...<br>...y ver un partido de fútbol. | I would love to visit a stadium...<br>...and watch a football match. |
| Me imagino que sería divertido...<br>...si tu equipo marca muchos goles. | I imagine it would be fun...<br>...if your team scores lots of goals. |
| El año pasado, mi equipo preferido ganó el campeonato de rugby. | Last year, my favourite team won the rugby championship. |
| Fue muy emocionante cuando el capitán alzó la copa. | It was very exciting when the captain lifted the trophy. |

## El deporte en la tele

Soy aficionado al baloncesto. Intento ver tantos partidos como sea posible.
**I am a fan of basketball. I try to watch as many games as possible.**

Prefiero jugar al hockey que verlo en la tele. En vez de pasar mucho tiempo viendo la tele, pienso que los jóvenes deberían practicar deporte.
**I prefer playing hockey to watching it on TV. Instead of spending a lot of time watching TV, I think young people should do sport.**

Me gusta ver torneos de tenis. Annette Setter es la actual campeona. Es una jugadora impresionante porque casi nunca pierde.
**I like watching tennis tournaments. Annette Setter is the reigning champion. She's an impressive player because she hardly ever loses.**

Me encanta ver los Juegos Olímpicos porque es interesante ver deportes menos populares como el piragüismo. Sueles aprender algo sobre ellos.
**I love watching the Olympic Games because it's interesting to watch less popular sports like canoeing. You usually learn something about them.**

# Technology

## La tecnología

| Mi madre usa el ordenador para descargar canciones. | My mum uses the computer to download songs. |
|---|---|
| Utilizo un portátil para hacer mis deberes. | I use a laptop to do my homework. |
| ¿Para qué usas tu móvil? | What do you use your mobile for? |
| Sin mi móvil, no podría... ...ni mandar ni recibir mensajes. ...hablar con mis amigos. | Without my mobile, I couldn't... ...send or receive messages. ...talk to my friends. |

## La red

Me encanta navegar por la red y creo que es crucial para la vida moderna.
**I love surfing the Internet and I think it's crucial for modern life.**

Es mucho más cómodo hacer las compras en línea.
**It's a lot more convenient to do your shopping online.**

La red es una herramienta muy útil porque puedes usar un buscador para encontrar información.
**The Internet is a very useful tool because you can use a search engine to find information.**

Me gustan los videojuegos porque puedes comunicarte con otros usuarios.
**I like video games because you can communicate with other users.**

Muchos internautas usan la red para sus cuentas bancarias porque es más fácil que ir al banco.
**Many Internet users use the web for their bank accounts because it's easier than going to the bank.**

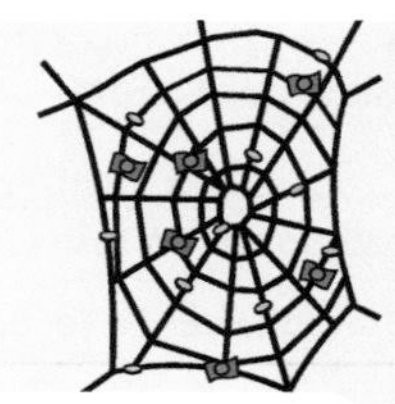

Leo los correos electrónicos en un navegador en lugar de una aplicación.
**I read emails in a browser instead of an application.**

# Technology

## Lo malo de la tecnología

Lo peor de los móviles es que la gente puede grabar vídeos sin informarte y compartir tus fotos con otra gente a la que no conoces.
**The worst thing about mobiles is that people can record videos without telling you and share your photos with other people you don't know.**

Lo más irritante es cuando mis amigos se enfadan porque no contesto a sus mensajes enseguida.
**The most irritating thing is when my friends get angry because I don't reply to their messages straightaway.**

No puedes escapar de la tecnología. Siempre tienes que estar conectado.
**You can't escape from technology. You always have to be connected.**

Creo que la tecnología puede ser adictiva.
Es importante desconectarse de vez en cuando.
**I think that technology can be addictive.**
**It's important to disconnect from time to time.**

## Protegerse en línea

| | |
|---|---|
| Hay que proteger tu identidad con una contraseña segura. | You must protect your identity with a strong password. |
| Si alguien averigua tu contraseña... ...puede acceder a tus archivos... ...y estropear tu disco duro. | If someone finds out your password... ...they can access your files... ...and ruin your hard disk. |
| También deberías borrar el correo basura del buzón... ...porque la gente puede adjuntar un virus... ...que daña tu ordenador. | You should also delete spam from your inbox... ...because people can attach a virus... ...that harms your computer. |
| Un buen servidor de seguridad te protegerá de estas amenazas. | A good firewall will protect you from these threats. |

# Social Media

## Las redes sociales

| Uso las redes sociales para... | I use social networks to... |
|---|---|
| ...charlar con mis primos en India. | ...chat with my cousins in India. |
| ...compartir fotos con mis amigos. | ...share photos with my friends. |
| ...leer blogs sobre mis intereses. | ...read blogs about my interests. |
| ...colgar recetas en algunos sitios web. | ...post recipes on some websites. |
| ...ver vídeos sobre música. | ...watch videos about music. |

Mis padres tienen miedo de las redes sociales ya que no las entienden.
**My parents are scared of social networks as they don't understand them.**

## Las ventajas y desventajas

Gracias a las redes sociales, sé lo que está pasando en el mundo.
**Thanks to social networks, I know what's happening in the world.**

No te aburres nunca y siempre hay algo que hacer.
**You never get bored and there's always something to do.**

Es muy fácil mantenerte en contacto con los amigos pero es importante salir con ellos también.
**It's very easy to keep in contact with your friends but it's important to go out with them too.**

Por una parte, siempre hay alguien con quien puedo charlar.
Por otra parte, las salas de chat pueden ser peligrosas.
**On one hand, there's always someone I can chat to.**
**On the other hand, chat rooms can be dangerous.**

Debido a las redes sociales, pierdo tiempo mirando cosas inútiles.
**Due to social networks, I waste time looking at useless things.**

La gente te puede mentir. Por eso, voy a desactivar mi cuenta.
**People can lie to you. Therefore, I'm going to deactivate my account.**

Diría que la gente pasa demasiado tiempo en las redes sociales.
**I would say that people spend too much time on social networks.**

# Customs and Festivals

## ¡Celebremos!

| | | | |
|---|---|---|---|
| ¡Feliz cumpleaños! | *Happy Birthday!* | tener suerte | *to be lucky* |
| ¡Felicitaciones! | *Congratulations!* | festejar | *to celebrate* |
| ¡Feliz año nuevo! | *Happy New Year!* | el día festivo | *public holiday* |
| el Año Nuevo | *New Year* | el santo | *saint's day* |

En Argentina, se celebra la fecha patria el 9 de julio.
**In Argentina, national independence day is celebrated on 9th July.**

'La Tomatina' tiene lugar en agosto en Buñol, Valencia y atrae a miles de turistas. Los participantes se lanzan tomates los unos a los otros.
**'La Tomatina' takes place in August in Buñol, Valencia and attracts thousands of tourists. Participants throw tomatoes at each other.**

En Nochevieja en España, se comen 12 uvas para traer buena suerte.
**On New Year's Eve in Spain, 12 grapes are eaten to bring good luck.**

## San Fermín

The running of the bulls happens at the festival of San Fermín.

Muchas personas corren por las calles estrechas de Pamplona con los toros peligrosos hasta la plaza de toros.
**Many people run through the narrow streets of Pamplona with the dangerous bulls to the bullring.**

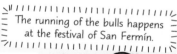

Los habitantes y los turistas llevan ropa blanca y pañuelos rojos.
**Locals and tourists wear white clothes and red scarves.**

La corrida de toros es una tradición común en España, y los toreros son admirados por muchas personas.
**Bullfighting is a common tradition in Spain, and bullfighters are admired by many people.**

Es polémica porque alguna gente piensa que es cruel matar animales por diversión.
**It is controversial because some people think that it's cruel to kill animals for fun.**

# Customs and Festivals

## El Día de los Muertos

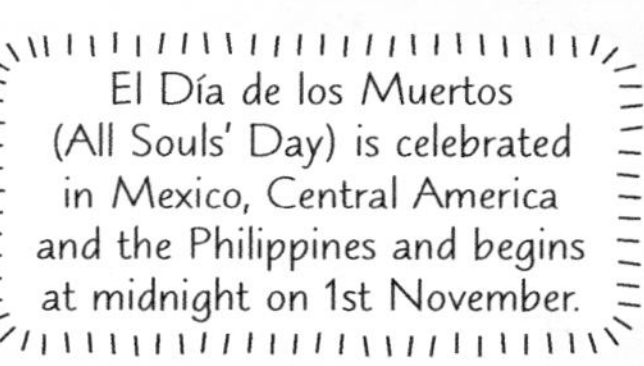


La gente cree que los difuntos reciben permiso para regresar durante 24 horas.
**People believe the dead receive permission to return for 24 hours.**

En la tradición mexicana, la muerte no es aterradora y se celebran las vidas de los muertos.
**In Mexican tradition, death isn't frightening and the lives of the dead are celebrated.**

'la Catrina' is a popular female skeleton icon.

| | |
|---|---|
| Alguna gente lleva maquillaje como y se disfraza de 'la Catrina'. | Some people wear make-up like and dress up as 'la Catrina'. |
| Honran a los muertos con calaveras de azúcar, flores y música del mariachi. | They honour the dead with sugar skulls, flowers and Mexican music. |
| Las familias limpian y arreglan las tumbas de sus parientes y amigos. | Families clean and tidy the graves of their relatives and friends. |

## El Día de los Inocentes

**El Día de los Inocentes se celebra el 28 de diciembre.**
**El Día de los Inocentes is celebrated on 28th December.**

| | |
|---|---|
| Es un día lleno de bromas. | It's a day full of jokes. |
| Es tradicional gastar una broma a alguien, por ejemplo...<br>...sustituir el azúcar por la sal.<br>...cambiar la hora del reloj. | It's traditional to play a joke on someone, for example...<br>...substitute sugar with salt.<br>...change the time on the clock. |
| Los medios de comunicación presentan noticias falsas de broma. | The media feature false news stories as a joke. |

# Customs and Festivals

## Semana Santa

La Pascua es un evento sombrío con muchas costumbres.
**Easter is a sombre event with a lot of customs.**

La gente enciende velas en la iglesia durante la Misa de Pascua.
**People light candles in church during Easter Mass.**

Durante la Semana Santa, hay procesiones con música.
**During Holy Week, there are processions with music.**

Se llevan pasos por las calles y la gente lleva ropa que esconde sus identidades.
**Statues are carried around the streets and people wear clothes that hide their identities.**

## ¡Feliz Navidad!

| | |
|---|---|
| Me encanta cantar villancicos... ...y me gusta comer turrón. | I love singing Christmas carols... ...and I like to eat nougat. |
| El Papá Noel trae regalos a los niños. | Father Christmas brings the children presents. |
| En España, se celebra la Nochebuena... ...con una gran cena familiar. | In Spain, Christmas Eve is celebrated... ...with a big family dinner. |
| Muchos españoles celebran el Día de Reyes el 6 de enero. | Many Spaniards celebrate Epiphany on 6th January. |

## Otras fiestas religiosas

Durante el Ramadán, muchos musulmanes ayunan durante las horas de luz.
**During Ramadan, many Muslims fast during daylight hours.**
El Eid al-Fitr es una fiesta musulmana que marca el fin del mes de Ramadán.
**Eid al-Fitr is a Muslim festival that marks the end of the month of Ramadan.**

Muchos judíos celebran Hanukkah. Lo festejan durante ocho días.
**Many Jews celebrate Hanukkah. They celebrate it for eight days.**
Se encienden velas, se dan regalos y se comen alimentos fritos.
**Candles are lit, gifts are given and fried food is eaten.**

# Talking About Where You Live

## ¿Dónde vives?

| | | | |
|---|---|---|---|
| las afueras | ***outskirts*** | el mercado | ***market*** |
| el puerto | ***port / harbour*** | la peluquería | ***hairdresser's*** |
| el ayuntamiento | ***town hall*** | la carnicería | ***butcher's*** |
| el aparcamiento | ***parking*** | el estanco | ***tobacconist's*** |
| el parque | ***park*** | la librería | ***book shop*** |
| la mezquita | ***mosque*** | la pastelería | ***pastry shop*** |
| la biblioteca | ***library*** | la pescadería | ***fishmonger's*** |
| la fábrica | ***factory*** | la panadería | ***bakery*** |
| la comisaría | ***police station*** | la papelería | ***stationery shop*** |
| el teatro | ***theatre*** | Correos | ***Post Office*** |

| | |
|---|---|
| Vivo cerca de una ciudad. | I live near a city. |
| Vivo en un pueblo pequeñito. | I live in a really small town. |
| Preferiría vivir más cerca del mar... ...porque me encanta la vela. | I'd prefer to live closer to the sea... ...because I love sailing. |

## Háblame de tu pueblo

Creo que es mejor vivir en el campo que en la ciudad.
**I think it's better to live in the countryside than in the city.**

Mi ciudad tiene varios edificios bonitos. También hay un museo impresionante en el centro.
**My city has various pretty buildings. There's also an impressive museum in the centre.**

'tuviera' is the imperfect subjunctive of 'tener'.

Mi barrio sería casi perfecto si tuviera una bolera.
**My neighbourhood would be almost perfect if it had a bowling alley.**

En un mundo ideal, viviría lejos del centro comercial porque hay tanta gente.
**In an ideal world, I'd live far away from the shopping centre because there are so many people.**

# The Home

## Mi casa

| | | | |
|---|---|---|---|
| la planta baja | *ground floor* | el cuarto de baño | *bathroom* |
| la segunda planta | *second floor* | el suelo | *floor* |
| el sótano | *basement* | la alfombra | *carpet* |
| la escalera | *stairs* | la pared | *wall* |
| el comedor | *dining room* | mudarse (de casa) | *to move house* |

Vivo en una casa adosada.
**I live in a semi-detached house.**

Vivimos en un piso pequeño.
**We live in a small flat.**

Hay siete habitaciones en mi casa.
**There are seven rooms in my house.**

La habitación que más me gusta es el salón porque hay sillones cómodos y una estantería llena de libros.
**The room I like best is the lounge because there are comfortable armchairs and shelves full of books.**

| | |
|---|---|
| En mi casa, hay pocos muebles. | In my house, there's little furniture. |
| Hay una ducha y un aseo. | There's a shower and a toilet. |
| En mi dormitorio, hay... ...una cama, un armario, un espejo y una mesita. | In my bedroom, there is... ...a bed, a wardrobe, a mirror and a little table. |
| En la cocina, hay... ...un fregadero, una nevera, un microondas y un horno. | In the kitchen, there is... ...a sink, a fridge, a microwave and an oven. |

## Mi casa ideal

Mi casa ideal tendría muchos electrodomésticos y un jardín grande.
**My ideal house would have lots of electrical appliances and a big garden.**

La casa de mis sueños tendría una piscina de lujo.
Además, sería mejor si no tuviera que compartir mi habitación.
**The house of my dreams would have a luxury pool.**
**It would also be better if I didn't have to share my room.**

# What You Do at Home

## Un día típico

¿Qué haces por la mañana?
**What do you do in the morning?**

**Reflexive verbs let you say what you do to yourself.**

**Me pongo la bufanda.**
**I put on my scarf.**

**Se maquilla.**
**He/She puts on make up.**

Me despierto a las siete y luego me ducho.
**I wake up at seven o'clock and then I have a shower.**

No me levanto hasta las siete y media. Luego me lavo la cara y me visto rápidamente.
**I don't get up until half past seven. Then I wash my face and get dressed quickly.**

Me acuesto a las diez pero no me duermo hasta las once.
**I go to bed at ten but I don't go to sleep until eleven.**

## Las tareas domésticas

| | |
|---|---|
| Cada mañana, hago mi cama... ...y arreglo mi dormitorio. | Every morning, I make my bed... ...and I tidy my bedroom. |
| Después de comer, quito la mesa... ...y lavo los platos. | After eating, I clear the table... ...and I wash the dishes. |
| En el verano, corto el césped. | In the summer, I mow the lawn. |
| Saco la basura todos los lunes. | I take the rubbish out every Monday. |
| Espero que todos ayuden en casa. | I hope that everyone helps at home. |
| No me dejan poner la mesa... ...porque siempre rompo algo. | They don't let me lay the table... ...because I always break something. |
| Limpio el salón los domingos. | I clean the lounge on Sundays. |
| Me gusta pasar la aspiradora. | I like doing the vacuuming. |
| Hacemos las compras los sábados. | We do the shopping on Saturdays. |
| Paseo al perro después del colegio. | I walk the dog after school. |

# Clothes Shopping

## De compras

| | | | |
|---|---|---|---|
| los grandes almacenes | ***department store*** | la falda | ***skirt*** |
| la joyería | ***jeweller's*** | la camisa | ***shirt*** |
| estar de moda | ***to be in fashion*** | la camiseta | ***T-shirt*** |
| la ropa de marca | ***designer clothes*** | los vaqueros | ***jeans*** |
| los probadores | ***changing rooms*** | la rebeca | ***cardigan*** |
| las rebajas | ***the sales*** | los calcetines | ***socks*** |

Este vestido me queda grande.
Quisiera que me lo cambie.
**This dress is too big for me.**
**I'd like you to change it for me.**

Estoy buscando unos pendientes,
pero no quiero gastar demasiado.
**I'm looking for some earrings,**
**but I don't want to spend too much.**

Quisiera un collar y un bolso que no sean caros.
**I'd like a necklace and a bag which aren't expensive.**

Tuve que comprar un regalo para mi hermana, así que fui a la zapatería.
**I had to buy a present for my sister, so I went to the shoe shop.**

Ya que no había zapatillas de deporte, fui a otra tienda para comprarle una chaqueta de cuero.
**As there weren't any trainers, I went to another shop to buy her a leather jacket.**

## Me gustaría...

Me encanta aquel abrigo.
**I love that coat over there.**

¿Me lo puedo probar?
**Can I try it on?**

¿Hay otra talla?
**Is there another size?**

Me gustaría esta corbata.
**I would like this tie.**

Creo que me quedaría bien.
**I think it would suit me.**

## Devoluciones y quejas

| | |
|---|---|
| el/la vendedor/a | ***salesperson*** |
| el/la dependiente/a | ***sales assistant*** |
| a mitad de precio | ***half-price*** |
| el descuento | ***discount*** |
| quejarse | ***to complain*** |
| hacer cola | ***to queue*** |
| devolver | ***to return*** |
| reembolsar | ***to refund*** |
| estar rasgado/a | ***to be ripped*** |
| estar roto/a | ***to be broken*** |
| un agujero | ***a hole*** |
| una mancha | ***a stain*** |

# More Shopping

## En la tienda de comestibles

| | | | | | |
|---|---|---|---|---|---|
| pagar | ***to pay*** | el/la cajero/a | ***cashier*** | un pedazo | ***piece*** |
| en efectivo | ***cash*** | la cantidad | ***quantity*** | un bote | ***jar*** |
| la caja | ***till*** | un cartón | ***carton*** | lleno/a | ***full*** |
| el recibo | ***receipt*** | una lata | ***tin*** | vacío/a | ***empty*** |

| | |
|---|---|
| Quisiera un trozo de tarta... ...y una ración de queso de cabra. | I would like a slice of cake... ...and a portion of goat's cheese. |
| ¿Cuánto cuesta una caja? | How much does a box cost? |
| Necesitamos una bolsa de patatas. | We need a bag of potatoes. |
| Nos hacen falta unos tomates. | We need some tomatoes. |
| ¿Puede usted pesar estas peras? | Could you weigh these pears? |
| Deme dos kilos de naranjas... ...y doscientos gramos de harina. | Give me two kilos of oranges... ...and two hundred grams of flour. |
| ¿Puedo pagar con tarjeta de crédito? | Can I pay by credit card? |

## ¿Te gusta hacer las compras en la red?

**Hacer las compras en la red es fácil y resulta más barato. Además, no tienes que salir de casa porque hay un servicio de reparto a domicilio.**
**Shopping online is easy and turns out cheaper. Besides, you don't have to leave the house because there's a home delivery service.**

**Prefiero ir de compras en un centro comercial porque para mí, es mejor ver las cosas <u>antes de comprar</u>las.**
**I prefer to go shopping in a shopping centre because, for me, it's better to see things <u>before buying</u> them.**

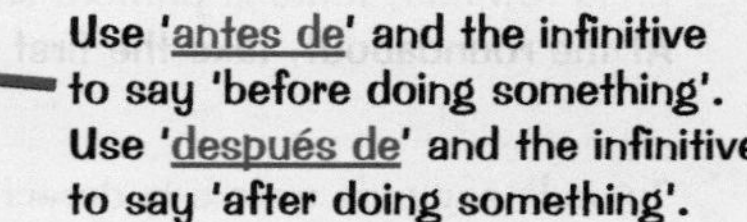

**Use '<u>antes de</u>' and the infinitive to say 'before doing something'. Use '<u>después de</u>' and the infinitive to say 'after doing something'.**

# Giving and Asking for Directions

## ¿Dónde está?

| | |
|---|---|
| El banco está al final de la calle. | The bank is at the end of the street. |
| La panadería está justo al lado de la piscina, enfrente del cine. | The bakery is right next to the swimming pool, opposite the cinema. |
| Está situado detrás del museo. | It's situated behind the museum. |
| Los servicios están en la esquina. | The toilets are on the corner. |
| Está delante de Correos. | It is in front of the Post Office. |

Es muy fácil encontrarlo/la.
**It's very easy to find it.**

Es bastante difícil verlo/la.
**It's quite difficult to see it.**

**Use the verb 'estar' to describe where things are. You can also use 'estar situado' to say where something is situated.**

## ¿Cómo se llega a...?

Siga todo recto y el ayuntamiento está entre la catedral y la biblioteca.
**Continue straight on and the town hall is between the cathedral and the library.**

Use the 'usted' form of the imperative to give instructions or directions to someone you don't know.

Tome esa calle y verá un semáforo. Luego gire a la izquierda. El parque está a la derecha del colegio.
**Take that road and you'll see some traffic lights. Then turn left. The park is on the right of the school.**

En la rotonda, tome la primera salida. El buzón está a la izquierda.
**At the roundabout, take the first exit. The post box is on the left.**

Tome la segunda calle a la derecha. Siga todo recto y cruce la calle.
**Take the second street on the right. Continue straight on and cross the street.**

# Weather

## Hace buen / mal tiempo

| Está... | It's... | | | Hace... | It's... |
|---|---|---|---|---|---|
| despejado | clear | caluroso | hot | sol | sunny |
| nublado | cloudy | fresco | fresh | viento | windy |
| lloviendo | raining | húmedo | humid | calor | hot |
| nevando | snowing | tormentoso | stormy | frío | cold |
| | | seco | dry | | |

| Hay... | There is / there are... |
|---|---|
| niebla | fog |
| hielo | ice |
| tormenta | a storm |
| chubascos | showers |

En el verano, hace buen tiempo.
**In summer, the weather is good.**

En el otoño, hace mal tiempo.
**In autumn, the weather is bad.**

El clima es húmedo en primavera.
**The climate is humid in spring.**

Nevará en Inglaterra este invierno.
**It will snow in England this winter.**

Consultaré el pronóstico.
**I will check the weather forecast.**

## ¿Qué tiempo habrá?

| | |
|---|---|
| Estará fresco por todas partes. | It will be fresh everywhere. |
| Hoy el cielo estará nublado. | Today the sky will be cloudy. |
| Hará mucho calor en el sur. | It will be very hot in the south. |
| Sería mejor si no hiciera tanto calor... ...porque prefiero el frío. | It would be better if it weren't so hot... ...because I prefer the cold. |
| Hoy hace mucho sol en el sur, pero mañana cambiará. | Today it's really sunny in the south, but tomorrow it will change. |
| Habrá truenos y relámpagos. | There will be thunder and lightning. |
| Mañana hará sol con la posibilidad de lluvia. | Tomorrow it will be sunny with the chance of rain. |

# Healthy and Unhealthy Living

## Una vida sana

| | |
|---|---|
| Para llevar una vida saludable...<br>...intento beber mucha agua.<br>...evito la comida basura.<br>...como poca comida rápida.<br>...como una dieta equilibrada.<br>...duermo al menos ocho horas cada noche. | In order to lead a healthy life...<br>...I try to drink lots of water.<br>...I avoid junk food.<br>...I eat little fast food.<br>...I eat a balanced diet.<br>...I sleep for at least eight hours each night. |
| Para mantenerme en forma, hago ejercicio casi todos los días. | To keep fit, I exercise almost every day. |
| Cuido de mi salud mental...<br>...relajándome después del colegio...<br>...y paseando cada día. | I look after my mental health...<br>...by relaxing after school...<br>...and going for a walk every day. |

## Una vida malsana

| | | | |
|---|---|---|---|
| el fumador (pasivo) | *(passive) smoker* | borracho/a | *drunk* |
| los espacios públicos | *public places* | el cigarrillo | *cigarette* |
| probar | *to try* | oler | *to smell* |
| la droga blanda / dura | *soft / hard drug* | el sobrepeso | *obesity* |
| emborracharse | *to get drunk* | cansarse | *to get tired* |

La gente que deja de fumar puede sufrir el síndrome de abstinencia.
**People who stop smoking can suffer withdrawal symptoms.**

Una vez, fui a un botellón, pero no me gustó.
**Once I went to a drinking party in the street, but I didn't like it.**

El tabaquismo me preocupa porque es peligroso.
**Addiction to tobacco worries me because it's dangerous.**

El humo hace daño a los pulmones y huele fatal.
**Smoke damages the lungs and it smells awful.**

# Illnesses

## Las enfermedades

| | | | |
|---|---|---|---|
| sentirse mal | *to feel ill* | seropositivo/a | *HIV-positive* |
| encontrarse / estar enfermo/a | *to be ill* | el cuerpo | *body* |
| mejorarse | *to get better* | el corazón | *heart* |
| el dolor | *pain* | el hígado | *liver* |
| el ataque cardíaco | *heart attack* | el cerebro | *brain* |
| el sida | *AIDS* | la depresión | *depression* |
| | | la ansiedad | *anxiety* |

**To say something hurts, use the verb 'doler' (to hurt). It works like 'gustar' — you need an indirect object pronoun before the verb and an 'n' in the plural.**

**Me duele la espalda.**
**My back hurts.**

**Me duelen los pies.**
**My feet hurt.**

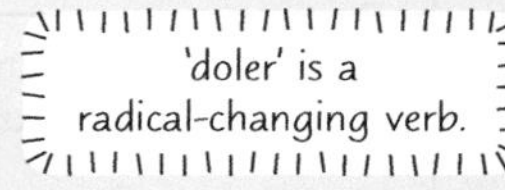
'doler' is a
radical-changing verb.

## Necesito ir al médico

| Hace un mes, me encontré mal y... ...tuve que ir al médico. ...el médico me dio una receta. | A month ago, I was ill and... ...I had to go to the doctor. ...the doctor gave me a prescription. |
|---|---|
| Tengo dolor de estómago. | I have stomach ache. |
| De niño, tenía muchos problemas respiratorios. | As a child, I had a lot of respiratory problems. |
| Creo que todos deberían hacer un curso de primeros auxilios. | I think everyone should do a first aid course. |
| La falta de médicos es un problema grave en algunos países. | The lack of doctors is a serious problem in some countries. |
| Muchos jóvenes se preocupan por... ...su peso y su apariencia. ...sus exámenes, lo que causa mucho estrés. | Lots of young people worry about... ...their weight and their appearance. ...their exams, which causes a lot of stress. |

# Environmental Problems

## El medio ambiente

| | | | |
|---|---|---|---|
| la capa de ozono | *ozone layer* | malgastar | *to waste* |
| los productos químicos | *chemicals* | el desperdicio | *wastage* |
| la lluvia ácida | *acid rain* | la escasez | *shortage* |
| dañar | *to damage* | la inundación | *flood* |
| echar la culpa | *to blame* | la sequía | *drought* |

| | |
|---|---|
| El cambio climático me preocupa. | Climate change worries me. |
| El uso de ciertos combustibles contamina el aire y causa el calentamiento global. | The use of certain fuels pollutes the air and causes global warming. |
| Debido al efecto invernadero, las temperaturas suben... ...lo que amenaza la supervivencia de algunos animales. | Due to the greenhouse effect, temperatures rise... ...which threatens the survival of some animals. |
| Los gases de escape son muy nocivos. | Exhaust fumes are very harmful. |

## La deforestación

Los bosques son importantes porque reducen la cantidad de dióxido de carbono en la atmósfera.
**Forests are important because they reduce the amount of carbon dioxide in the atmosphere.**

Hoy en día cortamos muchos árboles para producir combustibles o limpiar el terreno para la agricultura. Esto contribuye a la destrucción de los bosques, y al cambio climático.
**Nowadays we cut down lots of trees to produce fuel or to clear land for farming. This contributes to the destruction of forests, and to climate change.**

Si no actuamos ahora, las selvas y los bosques desaparecerán.
**If we don't act now, the jungles and forests will disappear.**

# Environmental Problems

## El desperdicio de agua

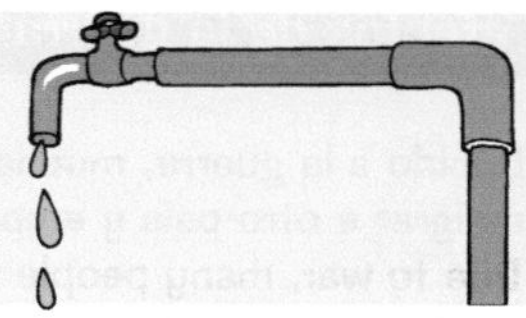

Debemos usar menos agua en nuestra vida diaria.
**We must use less water in our daily lives.**

El agua es necesaria para todo el mundo. Sin agua, los cultivos no pueden sobrevivir. Es un recurso importante que no deberíamos agotar.
**Water is necessary for everyone. Without water, crops can't survive. It's an important resource that we shouldn't use up.**

## La contaminación y otros problemas graves

Las mareas negras ensucian el mar y las playas. El petróleo es nocivo para los pájaros y las criaturas que viven en el mar.
**Oil spills make the sea and the beaches dirty. Oil is harmful for birds and the creatures that live in the sea.**

Es esencial que protejamos la naturaleza. Sin ella, no sobreviviremos.
**It's essential that we protect nature. Without it, we won't survive.**

Es importante que combatamos los efectos del cambio climático porque si no, vamos a sufrir en el futuro.
**It's important that we combat the effects of climate change because if not, we're going to suffer in the future.**

| | |
|---|---|
| Quiero que hagamos más para reducir la basura que producimos. | I want us to do more to reduce the rubbish that we produce. |
| Es muy fácil reciclar cartón y envases de plástico. | It's very easy to recycle cardboard and plastic packaging. |
| Si seguimos produciendo tanta basura... <br> ...todos los vertederos estarán llenos pronto. | If we continue producing so much rubbish... <br> ...all the rubbish tips will be full soon. |
| Es terrible que no pensemos más en las generaciones del futuro. | It's terrible that we don't think more about future generations. |

# Problems in Society

## Los efectos de la guerra

Debido a la guerra, muchas personas tienen que emigrar a otro país y empezar la vida de nuevo.
**Due to war, many people have to emigrate to another country and start their lives all over again.**

Use 'me parece' to say how something seems to you.

Desafortunadamente, hay prejuicio y discriminación contra los refugiados y los inmigrantes que vienen a vivir a este país.
**Unfortunately, there is prejudice and discrimination against refugees and immigrants who come to live in this country.**

No me parece justo que la libertad que tienes dependa tanto del país en que naciste.
**It seems unfair to me that the freedom you have depends so much on the country in which you were born.**

## La igualdad social

| | |
|---|---|
| Sería agradable creer que todos somos iguales, pero no es así. | It'd be nice to believe that we're all equal, but that's not the case. |
| La desigualdad crea una brecha entre los ricos y los pobres. | Inequality creates a gap between the rich and the poor. |
| Me encantaría vivir en una sociedad más justa. | I would love to live in a fairer society. |

## La violencia juvenil

En mi barrio, hay un grupo de jóvenes violentos que nos dan miedo.
**In my neighbourhood, there's a group of violent youths who scare us.**

Me enfadan mucho los grupos de gamberros que salen por la noche e intimidan a la gente mayor.
**The groups of troublemakers who go out at night and intimidate the older people make me really angry.**

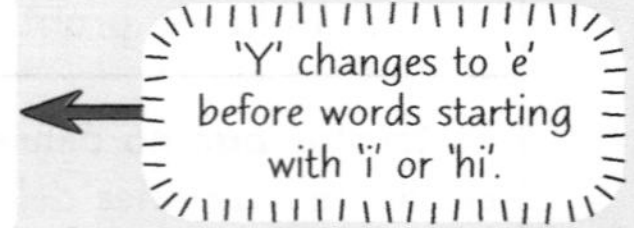

'Y' changes to 'e' before words starting with 'i' or 'hi'.

# Problems in Society

## La pobreza

| | |
|---|---|
| Creo que hay más pobreza que hace diez años. | I think there's more poverty than ten years ago. |
| El gobierno debería apoyar a los "sin techo". | The government should support homeless people. |
| Vivo en un país rico, pero todavía hay mucha gente sin comida. | I live in a rich country, but there are still lots of people without food. |
| Deberíamos luchar para ayudar a los más necesitados porque... ...es fácil acabar sin hogar o en la pobreza si pierdes tu trabajo. | We should fight to help the most needy people because... ...it's easy to end up homeless or in poverty if you lose your job. |
| La pobreza puede afectar a cualquier persona. | Poverty can affect anyone. |

## El desempleo

Mucha gente está en paro en mi ciudad.
**Lots of people are unemployed in my city.**

El desempleo es un peligro, especialmente para los jóvenes. Los expertos dicen que son los más afectados.
**Unemployment is a danger, especially for young people. The experts say they are the worst affected.**

Si pudiera cambiar algo, crearía más trabajos porque el desempleo es un gran problema que debemos solucionar.
**If I could change anything, I'd create more jobs because unemployment is a big problem that we must solve.**

Los que están en paro se encuentran en un círculo vicioso, ya que es más difícil encontrar otro trabajo si estás en paro.
**Those who are unemployed find themselves in a vicious circle, as it's harder to find another job if you're unemployed.**

# Contributing to Society

## Ser ecológico/a

Participé en una protesta en contra del uso de los combustibles fósiles.
**I participated in a protest against the use of fossil fuels.**

Deberíamos invertir en energía renovable para salvar el planeta.
**We should invest in renewable energy to save the planet.**

| Para proteger el medioambiente... | To protect the environment... |
|---|---|
| ...uso el transporte público. | ...I use public transport. |
| ...ahorro energía por apagar las luces. | ...I save energy by turning off the lights. |
| ...reutilizo las bolsas de la compra en vez de comprar nuevas. | ...I reuse shopping bags instead of buying new ones. |
| ...reciclo los desechos siempre que puedo. | ...I recycle rubbish whenever I can. |

## Ayudar a otros

Los domingos trabajo en una tienda solidaria y ayudo con el club de jóvenes en mi pueblo. Es esencial que hagamos algo por los demás.
**On Sundays I work in a charity shop and I help with the youth club in my town. It's essential that we do something for others.**

La soledad es un problema que afecta mucho a los ancianos. Todos deberíamos hacer más para cuidar de ellos.
**Loneliness is an issue that affects the elderly a lot. We should all do more to look after them.**

Acabo de lanzar una campaña para ayudar a las víctimas de desastres naturales como huracanes e incendios.
**I have just launched a campaign to help the victims of natural disasters like hurricanes and fires.**

Es importante que apoyemos a las organizaciones benéficas.
**It's important that we support charitable organisations.**

# Where to Go

## Los países y las nacionalidades

| | |
|---|---|
| Inglaterra | *England* |
| Escocia | *Scotland* |
| Gales | *Wales* |
| Irlanda del Norte | *Northern Ireland* |
| Gran Bretaña | *Great Britain* |
| Alemania | *Germany* |
| Italia | *Italy* |
| Europa | *Europe* |

Mi padre es medio irlandés, así que vamos a Irlanda a menudo.
**My father is half Irish, so we often go to Ireland.**

Soy griega y la mayoría de mi familia vive en Grecia.
**I'm Greek and most of my family live in Greece.**

Hace dos años, fui a los Estados Unidos y a Colombia con mis amigas escocesas.
**Two years ago, I went to the United States and Colombia with my Scottish friends.**

A mi hermana le encanta viajar. Ha viajado a Argentina, Perú y Chile. También le interesan la cultura brasileña y la comida mexicana.
**My sister loves travelling. She's travelled to Argentina, Peru and Chile. She's also interested in Brazilian culture and Mexican food.**

## ¿Adónde quisiera ir de vacaciones?

| | |
|---|---|
| Este verano, espero ir al norte de Francia y a Portugal. | This summer, I hope to go to the north of France and Portugal. |
| Me encantaría visitar Cuba... ...porque las playas son hermosas. | I'd love to visit Cuba... ...because the beaches are beautiful. |
| Australia es el destino de mis sueños... ...porque quiero ver la Gran Barrera de Coral. | Australia is my dream destination... ...because I want to see the Great Barrier Reef. |
| Quiero ir a Canadá para esquiar. | I want to go to Canada to ski. |
| Sueño con ir a la India... ...para ver elefantes salvajes. | I dream of going to India... ...to see wild elephants. |

# Accommodation

## El alojamiento

| | | | |
|---|---|---|---|
| el parador | ***state-owned hotel*** | un hotel de lujo | ***luxury hotel*** |
| las instalaciones | ***facilities*** | (irse de) camping | ***(to go) camping*** |
| la habitación doble | ***double room*** | la tienda | ***tent*** |
| la habitación individual | ***single room*** | el crucero | ***cruise*** |

## Quisiera alojarme en...

| | |
|---|---|
| Quisiera alojarme cuatro noches en una pensión. | I would like to stay for four nights in a boarding house. |
| Necesitamos una habitación...<br>...que tenga aire acondicionado.<br>...que tenga cuarto de baño. | We need a room...<br>...that has air-conditioning.<br>...that has a bathroom. |
| Preferiría una habitación...<br>...con vista al mar.<br>...con balcón.<br>...con cama de matrimonio. | I would prefer a room...<br>...with a sea view.<br>...with a balcony.<br>...with a double bed. |
| Me quedo en un albergue juvenil...<br>...para conocer a gente nueva.<br>...para ahorrar dinero. | I stay in a youth hostel...<br>...in order to meet new people.<br>...in order to save money. |
| Preferirían alojarse en un camping...<br>...porque tienen una caravana...<br>...y les gusta la naturaleza. | They'd prefer to stay on a campsite...<br>...because they have a caravan...<br>...and they like nature. |
| Mi amigo quisiera encontrar alojamiento de media pensión. | My friend would like to find half-board accommodation. |
| Preferiría reservar alojamiento de pensión completa. | I'd prefer to book full-board accommodation. |
| Por favor, ¿puedo reservar la mejor habitación disponible? | Please can I reserve the best room available? |

# Getting Ready and Getting There

## Las preparaciones

**Me informé del alojamiento disponible en la agencia de viajes.**
**I found out about the available accommodation at the travel agent's.**

**Ya he hecho mi maleta, pero todavía no he comprado una guía.**
**Necesito una que incluya información sobre Suiza e Italia.**
**I've already packed my suitcase but I haven't bought a guidebook yet.**
**I need one that includes information about Switzerland and Italy.**

**El guía nos dió unos folletos mientras nos mostraba las exposiciones.**
**The guide gave us some leaflets while showing us the exhibits.**

## Cómo llegar a tu destino

| | |
|---|---|
| El viaje a España fue largo... ...porque fuimos en coche. | The journey to Spain was long... ...because we went by car. |
| Tuvimos que parar en muchas estaciones de servicio para llenar el tanque con gasolina. | We had to stop at lots of service stations to fill the tank with petrol. |
| Me mareo en barcos... ...así que preferiría ir en avión. | I feel travel sick on boats... ...so I'd prefer to go by plane. |
| Compré un billete de ida y vuelta para ir a Toledo desde Madrid. | I bought a return ticket to go to Toledo from Madrid. |
| Exploré la ciudad a pie y fui en taxi al castillo. | I explored the city on foot and I went by taxi to the castle. |
| Me perdí en el Casco Histórico. | I got lost in the Old Town. |
| No me importa viajar en autocar pero prefiero el ferrocarril. | I don't mind travelling by coach but I prefer the railway. |
| El tranvía en Valencia te permite ver gran parte de la ciudad. | The tram in Valencia lets you see a lot of the city. |

# Getting There and What to Do

## Los problemas al viajar

Los pasajeros deben hacer transbordo en la próxima estación porque este tren ha sido cancelado.
**Passengers must change at the next station because this train has been cancelled.**

Coge el metro ya que hay un atasco en la autopista.
**Take the underground as there's a traffic jam on the motorway.**

El regreso será en autobús porque los empleados del aeropuerto están en huelga.
**The return will be by bus because the airport workers are on strike.**

El tren en este andén está retrasado una hora.
**The train on this platform is delayed by an hour.**

Perdí mi pasaporte antes del vuelo, así que tuve que alquilar un coche. Tuve que rellenar una ficha y mostrar mi carnet de conducir.
**I lost my passport before the flight, so I had to hire a car. I had to fill out a form and show my driving licence.**

## ¿Qué hiciste durante tus vacaciones?

| | | | |
|---|---|---|---|
| la excursión | ***trip, excursion*** | sacar / hacer fotos | ***to take photos*** |
| el recuerdo | ***souvenir*** | broncearse | ***to get a tan*** |
| caminar | ***to walk*** | el parque temático | ***theme park*** |
| esquiar | ***to ski*** | el parque de atracciones | ***fairground*** |

| | |
|---|---|
| Pasamos cada día en la playa... ...porque hacía sol. | We spent every day on the beach... ...because it was sunny. |
| Me bañé en el mar... ...y tomé el sol con mis primos. | I swam in the sea... ...and sunbathed with my cousins. |
| Me gusta nada más que probar nueva comida. | I like nothing more than trying new food. |
| También pasé mucho tiempo haciendo deportes acuáticos. | I also spent a lot of time doing water sports. |

# School Subjects and School Supplies

## Las asignaturas

| | | | |
|---|---|---|---|
| el español | ***Spanish*** | las matemáticas | ***maths*** |
| el alemán | ***German*** | el arte dramático | ***drama*** |
| el francés | ***French*** | las ciencias económicas | ***economics*** |
| el inglés | ***English*** | el comercio | ***business studies*** |
| las ciencias | ***science*** | la cocina | ***food technology*** |
| la biología | ***biology*** | los trabajos manuales | ***handicrafts*** |
| la física | ***physics*** | la gimnasia | ***gymnastics*** |
| la religión | ***RE*** | la educación física | ***PE*** |

| | |
|---|---|
| Mis asignaturas preferidas son... ...el dibujo y la informática... ...porque se puede ser creativo. | My favourite subjects are... ...art and IT... ...because you can be creative. |
| Me encanta la historia... ...porque es interesante y útil aprender sobre el pasado. | I love history... ...because it's interesting and useful to learn about the past. |
| Nos gusta la química... ...ya que es fascinante ver reacciones químicas. | We like chemistry... ...as it's fascinating to see chemical reactions. |
| Miguel odia la geografía... ...porque la encuentra aburrida. | Miguel hates geography... ...because he finds it boring. |

## En mi mochila

| | | | |
|---|---|---|---|
| la agenda | ***diary*** | el cuaderno | ***exercise book*** |
| el horario | ***timetable*** | el bolígrafo | ***pen*** |
| el libro | ***book*** | las tijeras | ***scissors*** |

This is often shortened to 'el boli'. (→ el bolígrafo)

| | |
|---|---|
| En mi mochila, hay un estuche. | In my school bag, there's a pencil case. |
| Se me ha olvidado mi lápiz. | I have forgotten my pencil. |
| ¿Me puedes prestar una regla? | Can you lend me a ruler? |

# School Routine

## Mi rutina escolar

| | |
|---|---|
| Mi colegio empieza a las nueve. | My school starts at nine o'clock. |
| Vamos al salón de actos y el profesor pasa la lista. | We go to the assembly room and the teacher calls the register. |
| Tengo cinco clases por día y cada clase dura cuarenta minutos. | I have five lessons a day and each lesson lasts forty minutes. |
| Durante el recreo... <br> ...juego al fútbol en el campo. <br> ...charlo con mis amigos. <br> ...prefiero ir a la biblioteca. | During break... <br> ...I play football on the field. <br> ...I chat with my friends. <br> ...I prefer to go to the library. |
| A la hora de comer... <br> ...almorzamos en la cantina. <br> ...nos sentamos juntos afuera. | At lunchtime... <br> ...we eat lunch in the canteen. <br> ...we sit outside together. |
| El día escolar termina a las cuatro. | The school day finishes at four. |
| Vuelvo a casa a las cuatro y diez. | I return home at ten past four. |
| Hay tres trimestres de cuatro meses en el año escolar. | There are three four-month-long terms in the school year. |

## Las reglas

Hay que levantar la mano antes de hablar.
**You have to raise your hand before speaking.**

Tienes que hacer deporte al menos tres veces a la semana.
**You have to do sport at least three times a week.**

No deberías ni comer chicle ni beber bebidas gaseosas.
**You shouldn't eat chewing gum or drink fizzy drinks.**

Es obligatorio llevar uniforme y no se puede llevar maquillaje.
**It's compulsory to wear a uniform and you can't wear make-up.**

# School Life and School Pressures

## ¿Cómo es tu colegio?

| | | | |
|---|---|---|---|
| la escuela primaria | ***primary school*** | el taller | ***workshop*** |
| la sala de profesores | ***staffroom*** | el aula (f) | ***classroom*** |
| el gimnasio | ***gymnasium*** | religioso/a | ***religious*** |
| los vestuarios | ***changing rooms*** | privado/a | ***private*** |

| | |
|---|---|
| Me llevo bien con los profesores. | I get on well with the teachers. |
| Hay instalaciones modernas tales como las pizarras interactivas. | There are modern facilities such as smart boards. |
| Es un instituto mixto y público con seiscientos alumnos. | It's a mixed state school with six hundred students. |

## El estrés y la vida escolar

| | | | |
|---|---|---|---|
| estresante | ***stressful*** | repasar | ***to revise*** |
| el éxito | ***success*** | el acoso | ***bullying*** |
| aprobar | ***to pass*** | el apoyo | ***support*** |
| suspender | ***to fail*** | apoyar | ***to support*** |

| | |
|---|---|
| Tengo demasiados deberes. | I have too much homework. |
| Hay mucha presión para sacar buenas notas. | There's a lot of pressure to get good marks. |
| Necesito sacar sobresalientes para ir a la universidad. | I need to get outstanding marks in order to go to university. |
| El mal comportamiento arruina las clases ya que es una distracción. | Bad behaviour ruins lessons as it is a distraction. |
| Algunos alumnos tienen una falta de respeto hacia los demás. | Some students have a lack of respect for others. |
| En mi colegio la intimidación es un problema muy grave... ...y las peleas ocurren a menudo. | In my school bullying is a serious problem... ...and fights happen often. |

# Education Post-16

## Cuando tenga 16 años...

**Quiero seguir mis estudios y hacer el bachillerato.**
**I want to continue my studies and do my A-levels.**

**Tengo la intención de ir a una academia para estudiar música.**
**I intend to go to an academy to study music.**

**Nuestra profesora recomienda que busquemos experiencia laboral.**
**Our teacher recommends that we look for work experience.**

**Hacer una práctica mejorará mis perspectivas laborales.**
**Doing a work placement will improve my work prospects.**

**Será desafiante, pero espero hacerme aprendiza de fontanero.**
**It'll be challenging, but I hope to become a plumber's apprentice.**

## Después del bachillerato...

| Voy a dedicarme a mis estudios...<br>...porque quiero conseguir un título.<br>...porque quiero ser traductor. | I'm going to focus on my studies...<br>...because I want to get a degree.<br>...because I want to be a translator. |
|---|---|
| Quisiera tomarme un año sabático antes de ir a la universidad. | I would like to take a gap year before going to university. |
| Quiero ser electricista, así que necesitaré formación profesional. | I want to be an electrician, so I will need professional training. |
| Se debe ir a la universidad si quieres hacer carrera en medicina. | You must go to university if you want to have a career in medicine. |
| Haré un aprendizaje para hacerme un carpintero calificado. | I will do an apprenticeship to become a qualified carpenter. |

# Career Choices and Ambitions

## Los empleos

abogado/a ***lawyer***
enfermero/a ***nurse***
veterinario/a ***vet***
jefe/a ***boss***
cocinero/a ***chef***
albañil ***builder***
bombero/a ***firefighter***
carpintero/a ***carpenter***
comerciante ***shop owner***
policía ***police officer***
camionero/a ***lorry driver***
pintor/a ***painter***

| Mi empleo ideal sería periodista, trabajando en una oficina. | My ideal job would be a journalist, working in an office. |
|---|---|
| Adjunto mi currículum para solicitar el puesto de contable. | I attach my CV to apply for the position of accountant. |
| Tengo un año de experiencia. | I have a year's experience. |
| Tengo una entrevista para el puesto de ingeniero. | I have an interview for the position of engineer. |
| Para mí, un trabajo debe ser... ...estimulante y gratificante. | For me, a job should be... ...stimulating and rewarding. |

## Un empleo a tiempo parcial

Tengo un empleo a tiempo parcial así que no recibo paga.
**I have a part-time job so I don't get pocket money.**

Lo mejor es que hay descuentos para los empleados.
**The best thing is that there are discounts for employees.**

Trabajo en una peluquería los sábados. Me gusta charlar con los clientes.
**I work in a hairdresser's on Saturdays. I like chatting with customers.**

Soy un camarero trabajador. Me gusta mi trabajo, pero no gano mucho.
**I'm a hard-working waiter. I like my job, but I don't earn a lot.**

Espero conseguir un trabajo variado que tenga un buen sueldo.
**I hope to find a varied job that has a good salary.**

# Words for People and Objects

## Gender of nouns

**Masculine nouns have 'el' or 'un' before them and are usually:**

| Nouns that end in: -o, -l, -n, -r, -s, -ta, -aje | Male people, days, months, languages, seas, rivers, oceans and mountains. |
|---|---|

el árbol — ***tree*** el atún — ***tuna*** el francés — ***French***

**Feminine nouns have 'la' or 'una' before them and are usually:**

| Nouns that end in: -a, -ción, -sión, -tad, -tud, -dad, -umbre | Female people, letters of the alphabet. |
|---|---|

la casa — ***house*** la canción — ***song*** la edad — ***age***

**You can't tell the gender of a noun ending in 'e' or 'ista'. You just have to learn them:**

| | | | |
|---|---|---|---|
| el coche | ***the car*** | el turista | ***the tourist (male)*** |
| la gente | ***the people*** | la turista | ***the tourist (female)*** |

**Common exceptions:**

| | | | | | |
|---|---|---|---|---|---|
| el día | ***day*** | el mapa | ***map*** | la moto | ***motorbike*** |
| el problema | ***problem*** | la foto | ***photo*** | la mano | ***hand*** |

## Making nouns plural

**To make most nouns that end in a vowel plural, just add 's'.** una cama → dos camas

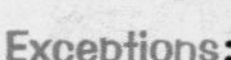

**Exceptions:**

1. **For nouns ending in consonants (not 'z'), add 'es'.** una flor → dos flores
2. **For nouns ending in 'z', drop the 'z' and add 'ces'.** un lápiz → dos lápices
3. **For days ending in 's' and surnames, only change the article.** el viernes → los viernes los Taylor

**You may need to add or remove an accent from some plurals to keep the pronunciation the same.** un inglés → dos ingleses

# 'The', 'A', 'Some' and Other Little Words

## Definite articles

Definite articles are for specific things — the dog(s), the door(s).

el perro los perros la puerta las puertas

'El' is also used for feminine nouns that start with a stressed 'a', e.g. 'el agua'.

You may need a definite article in Spanish when you wouldn't in English:

1. nouns used in a general sense — Me gusta el café. I like coffee.
2. days of the week and times — los lunes a las seis Mondays at six o'clock
3. weights and measurements — dos euros el kilo two euros a kilo
4. with a person's title — ¿Cómo está el señor Tan? How is Mr Tan?

Use 'lo' for things that aren't masculine or feminine. Any adjective that follows it should be masculine.

Lo peor es que... The worst thing is that...

## Indefinite articles

Indefinite articles refer to general things, e.g. a dog, some doors.

un perro unos perros una puerta unas puertas

Indefinite articles are left out after a negative verb, and after 'ser' when talking about someone's occupation or nationality.

Soy estudiante. I'm a student. No tengo perro. I haven't got a dog.

## Any, other, each, all

There's no special word for 'any' in Spanish. — ¿Tienes uvas? Have you got any grapes?

Use 'otro/a' for 'another'. You don't need 'un' or 'una' before it. — Lo haré otro día. I'll do it another day.

'Cada' means 'each'. It's the same for masculine and feminine nouns. — Cada otoño voy a Gales. Each autumn I go to Wales.

'Todo/a/os/as' means 'all'. — Compré todas las sillas. I bought all the chairs.

# Words to Describe Things

## Agreement

el chico bajo | la chica baja | los chicos bajos | las chicas bajas

**Adjectives that don't end in 'o' don't change in the singular. In the plural, add 's' if the adjective ends in a vowel, or 'es' if it ends in a consonant.**

la mujer triste
las mujeres tristes

**Some adjectives don't change to agree. Most of these are colours.**

| | | | |
|---|---|---|---|
| beis | *beige* | naranja | *orange* |
| lila | *lilac* | rosa | *pink* |

tres coches naranja
three orange cars

## Position and meaning

**Most adjectives go after the noun, but some always go in front of it:**

| | | | | | |
|---|---|---|---|---|---|
| mucho/a | *a lot of* | poco/a | *little* | primero/a, segundo/a... | *first, second...* |
| muchos/as | *lots of* | pocos/as | *few* | próximo/a | *next* |
| otro/a | *another* | tanto/a | *so much* | último/a | *last* |
| otros/as | *other* | tantos/as | *so many* | | |
| alguno/a | *some* | cada | *each* | | |

**'Bueno/a', 'primero/a', 'tercero/a', 'alguno/a', 'ninguno/a' and 'malo/a' all lose the final 'o' in front of a singular masculine noun. 'Alguno/a' and 'ninguno/a' also gain an accent on the 'u'.**

un buen día
a good day

**Position can change the meaning of some adjectives:**

'Grande' is the only adjective that drops 'de' in front of both masculine and feminine nouns.

| Before the noun... | After the noun... |
|---|---|
| un gran hombre — a great man | un hombre grande — a big man |
| el mismo día — the same day | yo mismo — I myself |
| un nuevo coche — a new (to owner) car | un coche nuevo — a brand new car |
| un viejo amigo — a long-standing friend | un amigo viejo — an old (elderly) friend |

# Words to Describe Things

## Possessive adjectives

These need to agree with the noun they're describing — not the person or thing that owns it.

tu gato    tus gatos

There are short and long forms of possessive adjectives. The short forms go before the noun, but the long forms (in brackets) go after it.

mi libro    el libro mío

| Possessive | Masc. sing. | Fem. sing. | Masc. pl. | Fem. pl. |
|---|---|---|---|---|
| my | mi (mío) | mi (mía) | mis (míos) | mis (mías) |
| your (inf. sing.) | tu (tuyo) | tu (tuya) | tus (tuyos) | tus (tuyas) |
| his / her / its / your (form. sing.) | su (suyo) | su (suya) | sus (suyos) | sus (suyas) |
| our | nuestro | nuestra | nuestros | nuestras |
| your (inf. pl.) | vuestro | vuestra | vuestros | vuestras |
| their / your (form. pl.) | su (suyo) | su (suya) | sus (suyos) | sus (suyas) |

## Other adjectives

Demonstrative adjectives are 'this', 'these', 'that', 'those', 'that over there', and 'those over there'. They need to agree with the noun they describe.

| | | | | | |
|---|---|---|---|---|---|
| este/a | *this* | ese/a | *that* | aquel(la) | *that over there* |
| estos/as | *these* | esos/as | *those* | aquellos/as | *those over there* |

este tigre
**this tiger**

esas faldas
**those skirts**

aquel coche
**that car over there**

aquella leche
**that milk over there**

'Cuyo' is a relative adjective and means 'whose'. It shows who something belongs to and agrees with the noun it is describing (not with the owner).

Es la chica cuy<u>o</u> gat<u>o</u> está allí.
**She is the girl whose cat is there.**

Es el hombre cuy<u>as</u> hij<u>as</u> conozco.
**He is the man whose daughters I know.**

# Words to Compare Things

## Comparatives and superlatives

más ... (que ...) **more ... (than ...)**

El piso es más barato que la casa.
**The flat is cheaper than the house.**

el más ... **the most ...**

El piso es el más barato.
**The flat is the cheapest.**

menos ... (que ...) **less ... (than ...)**

El piso es menos barato que la casa.
**The flat is less cheap than the house.**

el menos ... **the least ...**

El piso es el menos barato.
**The flat is the least cheap.**

tan ... como ... **as ... as ...**

El piso es tan barato como la casa.
**The flat is as cheap as the house.**

**The 'el' in 'el más' and 'el menos' has to agree with what it describes.**

Laura es la más baja.
**Laura is the shortest.**

Jo y Ed son los menos altos.
**Jo and Ed are the least tall.**

## Exceptions

**You don't use 'más' or 'menos' with these comparative and superlative forms:**

| Adjective | Comparative | Superlative |
|---|---|---|
| bueno (good) | mejor (better) | el mejor (the best) |
| malo (bad) | peor (worse) | el peor (the worst) |
| viejo (old) | mayor (older) | el mayor (the oldest) |
| joven (young) | menor (younger) | el menor (the youngest) |

**If the noun is feminine or plural, the superlative 'el' changes to agree. In the plural, you also need to add 'es' to the adjective.**

Lia y Aina son las mayores.
**Lia and Aina are the oldest.**

# Words to Describe Actions

## Forming adverbs

There are two ways to form adverbs in Spanish:

1. Add '-mente' to the end of a feminine adjective or an adjective that doesn't end in 'o'. → lentamente — **slowly**; fácilmente — **easily**

2. Use 'con' and a noun. → con cuidado — **with care / carefully**

Adverbs come after the verb, and they don't need to agree because they're describing an action.

## Exceptions

Use 'bien' to say 'well' and 'mal' to say 'badly'.

| | | | |
|---|---|---|---|
| bueno/a | *good* → | bien | *well* |
| malo/a | *bad* → | mal | *badly* |

As well as 'rápidamente' and 'lentamente', you can also use 'deprisa' and 'despacio' to say 'quickly' and 'slowly'.

## Adverbs of: 1 time, 2 place and 3 frequency

**1**

| | | | |
|---|---|---|---|
| de nuevo | *again* | de repente | *suddenly* |
| ya | *already* | ahora | *now / nowadays* |
| antes (de) | *before* | al mismo tiempo | *at the same time* |
| después (de) | *after* | de momento | *at the moment* |
| pronto | *soon* | en seguida | *straightaway* |
| todavía | *still, yet* | mientras tanto | *meanwhile* |

**2**

| | |
|---|---|
| aquí | *here* |
| ahí | *(just) there* |
| allá / allí | *(over) there* |
| cerca | *near* |
| lejos | *far away* |
| en / por todas partes | *everywhere* |

**3**

| | |
|---|---|
| a diario | *daily* |
| a menudo | *often* |
| a veces | *sometimes* |
| siempre | *always* |
| de vez en cuando | *from time to time* |
| pocas veces | *rarely, a few times* |

# Words to Compare Actions

## Comparatives

| | | |
|---|---|---|
| más ... (que ...) | more ... (than ...) | Eva trabaja más alegremente que Inés.<br>Eva works more happily than Inés. |
| menos ... (que ...) | less ... (than ...) | Inés trabaja menos alegremente que Eva.<br>Inés works less happily than Eva. |
| tan ... como ... | as ... as ... | Eva trabaja tan alegremente como Inés.<br>Eva works as happily as Inés. |

## Superlatives

To say someone does something 'the most / least ...ly', use:

**el / la / los / las + que + verb + más / menos + adverb**

Use either 'el', 'la', 'los' or 'las' to agree with the subject.

Juan es el que trabaja más alegremente.
**Juan works the most happily.**

Daniela es la que baila menos energéticamente.
**Daniela dances the least energetically.**

## Irregular forms

| Adverb | Comparative | Superlative |
|---|---|---|
| bien (well) | mejor (better) | el que mejor ... (the one who ... the best) |
| mal (badly) | peor (worse) | el que peor ... (the one who ... the worst) |

Cocino mejor que mis amigos. — **I cook better than my friends.**
Ellas son las que mejor juegan. — **They're the ones who play the best.**

Escribes peor que un niño. — **You write worse than a child.**
Él es el que peor canta. — **He's the one who sings the worst.**

# Words to Say How Much

## Quantifiers

Use quantifiers before nouns to say how much or how many. Most change their endings to agree with the noun, but 'un poco de' doesn't.

| | | | |
|---|---|---|---|
| mucho | *a lot / lots of* | demasiado | *too much / too many* |
| poco | *only a little / only a few* | tanto | *so much / so many* |
| un poco de | *a bit of* | bastante | *enough* |

Tenía muchos limones.
I had lots of lemons.

Hay tanta gente.
There are so many people.

Hay un poco de tarta.
There's a bit of pie.

You can also use quantifiers with verbs. They work like adverbs, so they go after the verb and they don't change their endings.

Hablas demasiado.
You talk too much.

Corre mucho.
She runs a lot.

## Intensifiers

Intensifiers strengthen what you're saying. They go before the word they're modifying, but their endings don't change at all.

Simón y Tia están muy felices.
Simón and Tia are very happy.

Es poco cortés.
He's not very polite.

Habla demasiado tranquilamente.
She speaks too quietly.

Comes bastante bien.
You eat quite well.

## Making adjectives seem smaller or stronger

You can add 'ito/a/os/as' to the end of most adjectives to make something seem smaller or cuter.

El bebé está enfermito.
The baby is poorly.

Add 'ísimo/a/os/as' to make the meaning of what you're saying stronger.

La película es malísima.
The film is terrible.

# I, You, We

## Subject and object

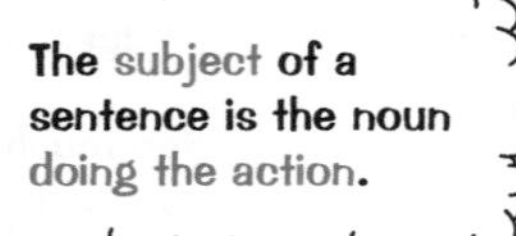

The subject of a sentence is the noun doing the action.


The object of a sentence is the noun having the action done to it.

'Pau' is the subject. → Pau come la pera. Pau eats the pear. ← 'The pear' is the object.

## I, you, he, she

**Pronouns replace nouns. They help to avoid repetition in sentences.**

**Subject pronouns are words like 'I', 'you', 'he' and 'she'. They're not normally used in Spanish because verb endings show who is doing an action.**

| I | yo | we | nosotros/as |
|---|---|---|---|
| you (inf. sing.) | tú | you (inf. pl.) | vosotros/as |
| he / it | él | they (masc.) | ellos |
| she / it | ella | they (fem.) | ellas |
| you (form. sing.) | usted | you (form. pl.) | ustedes |

The masculine 'they' form is also used for groups of masculine and feminine nouns.

## Emphasis

**Although you don't usually need subject pronouns in Spanish, they can help emphasise exactly who does what. They're used when extra stress is put on pronouns in English.**

¿Qué queréis hacer el fin de semana que viene?
**What would you (inf. pl.) like to do next weekend?**

Pues, yo quiero ir de compras, pero él quiere ir al cine.
**Well, I want to go shopping, but he wants to go to the cinema.**

# Me, You, Them

## Me, you, him, her

Use direct object pronouns to talk about who or what an action is done to. They usually go before the verb.

| me | me | us | nos |
|---|---|---|---|
| you (inf. sing.) | te | you (inf. pl.) | os |
| him / it | lo | them (masc.) | los |
| her / it | la | them (fem.) | las |
| you (form. sing.) | lo/la | you (form. pl.) | los/las |

Mika lava el perro.
Mika washes the dog.

Mika lo lava.
Mika washes it.

## To me, to you

Use indirect object pronouns to talk about doing something 'to' or 'for' someone. They're the same pronouns you use with the verb 'gustar'.

| to me | me | to us | nos |
|---|---|---|---|
| to you (inf. sing.) | te | to you (inf. pl.) | os |
| to him / her / it / you (form. sing.) | le | to them / you (form. pl.) | les |

El perro da el cepillo a Mika.
The dog gives the brush to Mika.

El perro le da el cepillo.
The dog gives the brush to him.

## Order of pronouns

Object pronouns can go before / after an infinitive or a present participle.
You often need to add an accent to keep the pronunciation the same.

Lo quiero ver. OR Quiero verlo.
I want to see it.

Le estoy hablando. OR Estoy hablándole.
I'm talking to him.

Pronouns go at the end of commands. Escríbeme. Write to me.

When two object pronouns come together, the indirect one comes first.
The pronouns 'le' or 'les' become 'se' in front of 'lo', 'la', 'los' or 'las'.

Dárselo. Give it to him / her / them / you (form.)

# More Pronouns

## Que

'Que' can mean 'that', 'which' or 'who' — it's a relative pronoun. Use it to start a relative clause, which is a way of adding detail to a sentence.

¿Dónde está el pan <u>que</u> compraste? **Where is the bread <u>that</u> you bought?**

To talk about an idea instead of an object, you need 'lo que'.

Van a venir, <u>lo que</u> es genial. **They're going to come, <u>which</u> is great.**

After prepositions, like 'con', 'a' and 'de', use 'quien(es)' for people (who) and 'el / la / los / las que' or 'el / la / los / las cual(es)' for other nouns (that / which).

el hombre <u>con quien</u> estoy hablando
**the man <u>with whom</u> I'm talking**

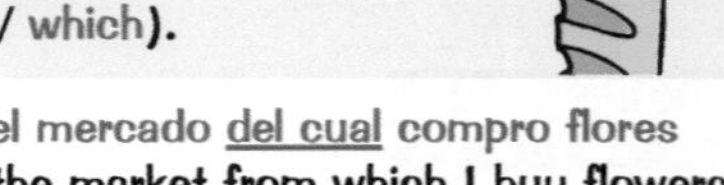

el mercado <u>del cual</u> compro flores
**the market <u>from which</u> I buy flowers**

## (With) me and (with) you

After prepositions like 'a', 'para', 'sobre' and 'de', the words for 'me' and 'you (inf. sing.)' become 'mí' and 'ti'. 'Mí' needs an accent.

Es para ti. **It's for you.**

'With me' becomes 'conmigo' and 'with you' becomes 'contigo'.

Está conmigo. **He's with me.**

## Indefinite pronouns

'Algo' (something) and 'alguien' (someone) are indefinite pronouns.

¿Quieren algo?
**Do they want something?**

Vi <u>a</u> alguien. **I saw someone.**

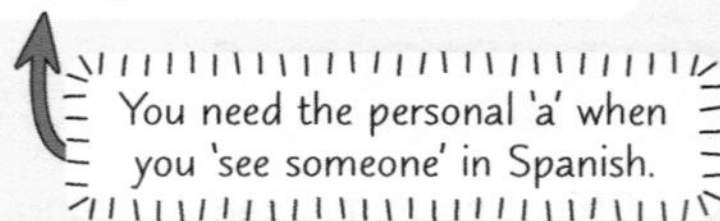

You need the personal 'a' when you 'see someone' in Spanish.


## Interrogative pronouns

Use '¿Qué...' (what) to ask about a specific thing or idea. Use '¿Cuál...' or '¿Cuáles...' (which) to distinguish between two or more things.

¿Qué haces? **What are you doing?**

¿Cuál es? **Which (one) is it?**

'¿Quién...' means 'Who...' and is often used with prepositions.

¿Con quién? **With whom?**

# More Pronouns

## Possessive pronouns

**Use possessive pronouns to say who something belongs to.**
**They agree in gender and number with the noun they're replacing.**

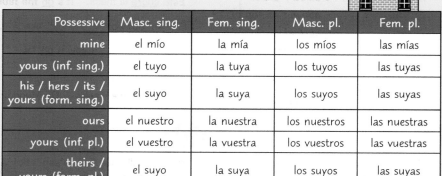

| Possessive | Masc. sing. | Fem. sing. | Masc. pl. | Fem. pl. |
|---|---|---|---|---|
| mine | el mío | la mía | los míos | las mías |
| yours (inf. sing.) | el tuyo | la tuya | los tuyos | las tuyas |
| his / hers / its / yours (form. sing.) | el suyo | la suya | los suyos | las suyas |
| ours | el nuestro | la nuestra | los nuestros | las nuestras |
| yours (inf. pl.) | el vuestro | la vuestra | los vuestros | las vuestras |
| theirs / yours (form. pl.) | el suyo | la suya | los suyos | las suyas |

¿Es tu casa? No, la mía es más alta. **Is it your house? No, mine is taller.**

¿Es su hotel? No, el nuestro está allí. **Is it your hotel? No, ours is there.**

## Demonstrative pronouns

Demonstrative pronouns **look the same as** demonstrative adjectives.
**Their endings** change to agree **with the noun they refer back to.**

| Demonstrative | Masc. sing. | Fem. sing. | Masc. pl. | Fem. pl. |
|---|---|---|---|---|
| this / these one(s) | este | esta | estos | estas |
| that / those one(s) | ese | esa | esos | esas |
| that / those one(s) over there | aquel | aquella | aquellos | aquellas |

Me gustaría este.
**I would like this one.**

Prefiere esas.
**She prefers those.**

Compré aquellos.
**I bought those over there.**

**Use the** neuter forms 'esto', 'eso' and 'aquello'
**if you** don't **know the** gender **of the noun.**

¿Qué es eso? **What's that?**

# Prepositions

## Common prepositions

| | |
|---|---|
| entre | *between* |
| bajo / debajo de | *below / under* |
| encima de | *above / on top of* |
| contra | *against* |
| al fondo de | *at the back of* |
| hacia | *towards* |
| sin | *without* |
| según | *according to* |

## Sobre, en

For 'on top of', use 'sobre' or 'en'.

Está sobre la mesa. It's on the table.

For 'on' but not 'on top of', use 'en'.

Lo vi en la tele. I saw it on TV.

You don't need 'en' for days of the week.

El lunes...
On Monday...

## De

Use 'de' to mean 'of' or to say what something is made of.

Es de oro. It's made of gold.

You can't say 'de el' (or 'a el'):

| | el | la |
|---|---|---|
| de | del | de la |
| a | al | a la |

## En, a

You normally use 'en' to say 'at', but sometimes you need 'a'.

Está en el cañón.
She's at the canyon.

a las seis — at six o'clock

al final de — at the end of

## En, dentro de

Use 'en' to say 'in' and 'dentro de' to say 'inside'. The verb 'entrar' is normally followed by 'en'.

En Leeds...
In Leeds...

dentro de la caja
inside the box

Entro en la tienda. I enter the shop.

## A, hasta

Use 'a' to say 'to'. When 'to' means 'as far as', use 'hasta'.

Va a Liverpool.
She is going to Liverpool.

Solo va hasta Manchester.
He is only going to Manchester.

## De, desde, a partir de

'From' is usually 'de'. Use 'desde' with a start and end point and 'a partir de' for dates.

Es de Kent.
He's from Kent.

desde Fife hasta Ayr
from Fife to Ayr

a partir de julio
from July

# 'Por', 'Para' and the Personal 'a'

## Use 'por' to...

1. ...talk about past duration. — Vivió allí por un año. **He lived there for a year.**
2. ...talk about parts of the day. — por la mañana **in the morning**
3. ...say 'through'. — Entré por la puerta. **I came through the door.**
4. ...say 'per' or 'a' in number phrases. — una vez por día **once a day**
5. ...talk about exchanges. — Pagué por el té. **I paid for the tea.**
6. ...say 'on behalf of'. — Lo hice por ti. **I did it for you.**
7. ...say 'thank you'. — Gracias por el boli. **Thanks for the pen.**

## Use 'para' to...

1. ...say who something is for. — Este bote es para ti. **This jar is for you.**
2. ...talk about destinations. — el tren para Bilbao **the train for Bilbao**
3. ...say 'to' or 'in order to'. — Corro para descansar. **I run to relax.**
4. ...say 'by' in time phrases. — para mañana **by tomorrow**
5. ...talk about future duration. — Lo quiero para un día. **I want it for one day.**
6. ...give an opinion. — Para mí, es bonito. **For me, it's pretty.**
7. ...say 'about to'. — Está para llover. **It's about to rain.**

## The personal 'a'

**You need an extra 'a' before the word for any human being or pet after almost every verb.**

Estoy buscando a Rhea.
I'm looking for Rhea.

**BUT**

Estoy buscando un taxi.
I'm looking for a taxi.

You don't usually use the personal 'a' after 'tener' or 'ser'.

# Conjunctions

## Y

'Y' means 'and'.

Juego al fútbol y al rugby.
I play football and rugby.

'Y' changes to 'e' before a word starting with 'i' or 'hi'.

Hablo español e inglés.
I speak Spanish and English.

## O

'O' means 'or'.

Juego al fútbol o al rugby los sábados.
I play football or rugby on Saturdays.

'O' changes to 'u' before a word starting with 'o' or 'ho'.

Cuesta siete u ocho euros.
It costs seven or eight euros.

## Pero

'Pero' means 'but'.

Me gusta el fútbol, pero no me gusta el rugby.
I like football, but I don't like rugby.

Use 'sino' when you want to say 'but rather'.

No es español, sino francés.
He isn't Spanish, but (rather) French.

## Porque

'Porque' helps you give opinions.

Me gusta porque es sabroso.
I like it because it's tasty.

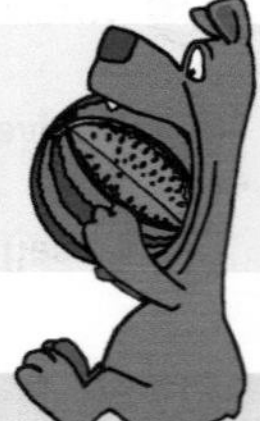

## Other common conjunctions

| | | | |
|---|---|---|---|
| sin embargo | *however* | ya que | *as, because* |
| así que | *so, therefore* | pues | *well, then* |
| de manera que | *such that* | entonces | *then* |
| mientras | *while* | si | *if* |
| como | *as, since* | cuando | *when* |

# Verbs in the Present Tense

## Forming the present tense

Most regular verbs in Spanish end in '-ar', '-er' or '-ir'.
To form the present tense, you need to find the stem.
To do this, remove the last two letters from the infinitive. hablar → habl-

Then add the endings below to the stem:

| -ar verbs, e.g. 'hablar' | |
|---|---|
| hablo | hablamos |
| hablas | habláis |
| habla | hablan |

Cantan bien.
They sing well.

Echo la pelota.
I throw the ball.

| -er verbs, e.g. 'comer' | |
|---|---|
| como | comemos |
| comes | coméis |
| come | comen |

Bebes té.
You drink tea.

Vendemos uvas.
We sell grapes.

| -ir verbs, e.g. 'vivir' | |
|---|---|
| vivo | vivimos |
| vives | vivís |
| vive | viven |

Interrumpís.
You interrupt.

Linh escribe una carta.
Linh writes a letter.

## Use the present tense...

1. ...for actions taking place now. Estudio español. I study Spanish.
2. ...for things that take place regularly. Cocino cada día. I cook every day.
3. ...with 'desde hace' to say how long you've been doing something.
   Toco el violín desde hace un año. I've been playing the violin for one year.
4. ...for things that are about to happen. Mañana vamos a la playa. Tomorrow we are going to the beach.

# Irregular Verbs in the Present Tense

## Radical-changing verbs

These verbs use regular verb endings but change their spelling in the present tense in every form apart from the 'we' and 'you (inf. pl.)' forms.

The 'e' to 'i' change only happens in '-ir' verbs.

| 'e' to 'ie', e.g. querer | |
|---|---|
| quiero | queremos |
| quieres | queréis |
| quiere | quieren |

| 'o/u' to 'ue', e.g. poder | |
|---|---|
| puedo | podemos |
| puedes | podéis |
| puede | pueden |

| 'e' to 'i', e.g. pedir | |
|---|---|
| pido | pedimos |
| pides | pedís |
| pide | piden |

**Other 'e' to 'ie' verbs:**

| | |
|---|---|
| cerrar | *to close* |
| comenzar | *to begin* |
| empezar | *to begin* |
| pensar | *to think* |
| preferir | *to prefer* |
| sentir(se) | *to feel* |
| tener | *to have* |
| venir | *to come* |

**Other 'o/u' to 'ue' verbs:**

| | |
|---|---|
| costar | *to cost* |
| doler | *to hurt* |
| dormir | *to sleep* |
| encontrar | *to find* |
| jugar | *to play* |
| llover | *to rain* |
| morir | *to die* |
| volver | *to return* |

**Other 'e' to 'i' verbs:**

| | |
|---|---|
| conseguir | *to achieve* |
| corregir | *to correct* |
| elegir | *to choose* |
| medir | *to measure* |
| repetir | *to repeat* |
| seguir | *to follow* |
| servir | *to serve* |
| sonreírse | *to smile* |

The first person singular forms of 'tener' and 'venir' are irregular.

## Common irregular verbs

**Irregular forms:**

'Ir' (to go): completely irregular.

| | |
|---|---|
| voy | vamos |
| vas | vais |
| va | van |

'Dar' (to give): the 'I' form ('doy') and the 'you (inf. pl.)' form ('dais').

Te doy el libro. I give you the book.

'Hacer' (to do / make): the 'I' form ('hago').

Hago la cama. I make the bed.

'Saber' (to know, e.g. a fact): the 'I' form ('sé').

Sé su edad. I know her age.

'Conocer' (to know, e.g. a person): the 'I' form ('conozco').

Conozco a Abir. I know Abir.

# 'Ser' and 'Estar' in the Present Tense

## 'Ser' means 'to be'

'Ser' is for permanent things.
It's a completely irregular verb.

| ser (to be) | |
|---|---|
| soy | somos |
| eres | sois |
| es | son |

Use it to...

1. ...talk about nationalities. — Somos galeses. **We are Welsh.**
2. ...say someone's name or who they are. — Nerea es mi prima. **Nerea is my cousin.**
3. ...talk about someone's job. — Mi tío es profesor. **My uncle is a teacher.**
4. ...describe physical characteristics. — Sois altos. **You (inf. pl.) are tall.**
5. ...describe someone's personality. — Son alegres. **They are cheerful.**

## 'Estar' means 'to be'

'Estar' is for temporary things and locations. It's a completely irregular verb.

| estar (to be) | |
|---|---|
| estoy | estamos |
| estás | estáis |
| está | están |

Use it to...

1. ...talk about things that might change in the future.

   Estoy bastante enfermo. **I'm quite ill.**

   Estás muy triste. **You are very sad.**

2. ...talk about where someone or something is.

   Madrid está en España. **Madrid is in Spain.**

   Estamos en casa. **We are at home.**

# Talking About the Past

## The preterite tense

To form the preterite tense of regular verbs, find the stem and then add these endings:

| -ar verbs | |
|---|---|
| -é | -amos |
| -aste | -asteis |
| -ó | -aron |

| -er and -ir verbs | |
|---|---|
| -í | -imos |
| -iste | -isteis |
| -ió | -ieron |

Cocinaron el arroz.
**They cooked the rice.**

Abrí la ventana.
**I opened the window.**

## Irregular verbs

'Ser', 'ir', 'estar' and 'hacer' are the four most important irregular verbs in the preterite tense. 'Ser' and 'ir' are the same in the preterite tense.

| ser (to be), ir (to go) | |
|---|---|
| fui | fuimos |
| fuiste | fuisteis |
| fue | fueron |

| estar (to be) | |
|---|---|
| estuve | estuvimos |
| estuviste | estuvisteis |
| estuvo | estuvieron |

| hacer (to do / make) | |
|---|---|
| hice | hicimos |
| hiciste | hicisteis |
| hizo | hicieron |

Verbs ending in '-car' change their 'c' to 'qu' in the 'I' form. tocar → toqué

Verbs ending in '-zar' change their 'z' to 'c' in the 'I' form. cruzar → crucé

Some verbs change their stem in the preterite tense, and they also lose the accent on their 'I' and 'he/she/it/you (form. sing.)' forms.

| | |
|---|---|
| dar (to give) | di- |
| decir (to say) | dij- |
| poder (to be able to) | pud- |
| poner (to put) | pus- |

| | |
|---|---|
| querer (to want) | quis- |
| tener (to have) | tuv- |
| traer (to bring) | traj- |
| venir (to come) | vin- |

Lo pusimos en la mesa.
**We put it on the table.**

Viniste a la fiesta.
**You came to the party.**

Mia me dio un gato.
**Mia gave me a cat.**

# Talking About the Past

## The imperfect tense

To form the imperfect tense, find the stem and then add these endings:

| -ar verbs | |
|---|---|
| -aba | -ábamos |
| -abas | -abais |
| -aba | -aban |

| -er and -ir verbs | |
|---|---|
| -ía | -íamos |
| -ías | -íais |
| -ía | -ían |

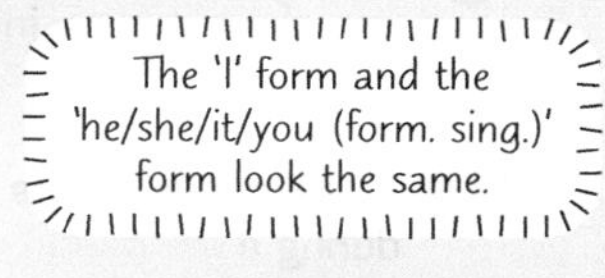

The 'I' form and the 'he/she/it/you (form. sing.)' form look the same.


Hablaba con Iratxe.
**I was talking to Iratxe.**

Iris tenía hambre.
**Iris was hungry.**

Estabas en el cine.
**You were at the cinema.**

Vivíamos allí.
**We used to live there.**

## Irregular verbs

'Ser' and 'ir' are completely irregular. 'Ver' uses the regular imperfect tense endings but has an irregular stem, 've-'.

| ser (to be) | |
|---|---|
| era | éramos |
| eras | erais |
| era | eran |

| ir (to go) | |
|---|---|
| iba | íbamos |
| ibas | ibais |
| iba | iban |

| ver (to see) | |
|---|---|
| veía | veíamos |
| veías | veíais |
| veía | veían |

Mi padre era pintor.
**My dad was a painter.**

Íbamos al concierto.
**We went to the concert.**

Veía la tele.
**I used to watch TV.**

## Había

'Había' is the imperfect form of 'hay'. It means 'there was' or 'there were'.

'Hay' and 'había' come from the verb 'haber'.

It stays the same regardless of whether the noun is singular or plural.

<u>Había</u> un mono en el árbol.
**<u>There was</u> a monkey in the tree.**

Siempre <u>había</u> muchos niños allí.
**<u>There were</u> always lots of children there.**

# Talking About the Past

## Use the preterite tense to...

1. ...talk about a single completed action in the past.

   Fui a la playa el jueves.
   I went to the beach on Thursday.

2. ...talk about events that happened during a set period of time.

   Ayer hizo calor.
   Yesterday it was hot.

3. ...interrupt a description of movement taking place in the imperfect tense.

   Volvía del gimnasio cuando vi a Delaram.
   I was coming back from the gym when I saw Delaram.

## Use the imperfect tense to...

1. ...talk about what you used to do repeatedly in the past.

   Iba a la playa cada día.
   I used to go to the beach every day.

   You can also use 'solía' (the imperfect tense of 'soler') and an infinitive to say what you used to do.

   Solía ir a la playa cada día. I used to go to the beach every day.

2. ...describe something, like the weather, in the past.

   Hacía calor, pero estaba nublado.
   It was hot, but it was cloudy.

3. ...say where you were going when something else happened.

   Volvía del gimnasio cuando vi a Delaram.
   I was coming back from the gym when I saw Delaram.

4. ...say how long something had been happening for with 'desde hacía' (the imperfect form of 'desde hace').

   Leía desde hacía una hora cuando me llamó.
   I had been reading for an hour when he called me.

# Talking About the Past

## Past participles

In the sentence 'I have done', 'done' is a past participle.
Past participles don't have to agree when used as part of a tense.
To form a past participle, find the stem, then add these endings:

| -ar verbs | -ado |
|---|---|
| hablar | hablado |

| -er verbs | -ido |
|---|---|
| beber | bebido |

| -ir verbs | -ido |
|---|---|
| elegir | elegido |

There are some irregular participles that you also need to learn:

| | | | |
|---|---|---|---|
| abrir | abierto (opened) | leer | leído (read) |
| cubrir | cubierto (covered) | poner | puesto (put) |
| decir | dicho (said) | romper | roto (broken) |
| escribir | escrito (written) | ver | visto (seen) |
| hacer | hecho (done / made) | volver | vuelto (returned) |

## The perfect tense

Use the perfect tense to talk about what you 'have done'.
You need the present tense of the verb 'haber' and a past participle.

| haber — present tense | |
|---|---|
| he | hemos |
| has | habéis |
| ha | han |

Han jugado al tenis. They have played tennis.

¡Ojas ha roto la llave! Ojas has broken the key!

## The pluperfect tense

Use the pluperfect tense to talk about what you 'had done'.
You need the imperfect tense of the verb 'haber' and a past participle.

| haber — imperfect tense | |
|---|---|
| había | habíamos |
| habías | habíais |
| había | habían |

Había comprado un gato. She had bought a cat.

Habían visto el coche. They had seen the car.

# Talking About the Future

## The immediate future tense

**Use the immediate future tense to talk about what's about to happen as well as something further in the future.**

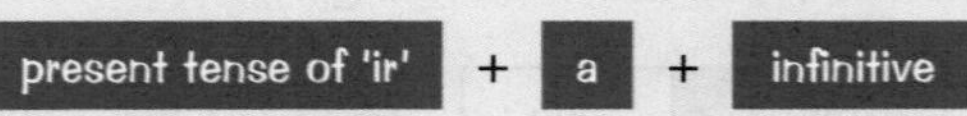


Me voy a comer la pera.
**I'm going to eat the pear.**

Susana va a leer una revista.
**Susana is going to read a magazine.**

**Add time phrases to say when you're going to do something.**

El lunes, vamos a ir a Francia.
**On Monday, we're going to go to France.**

Mañana voy a nadar.
**Tomorrow I'm going to swim.**

## The proper future tense

**Use the proper future tense to say what will happen.**

infinitive + future tense endings

| -ar, -er and -ir verbs | |
|---|---|
| -é | -emos |
| -ás | -éis |
| -á | -án |

Jugaré al tenis. **I will play tennis.**

Cogerá el autobús. **He will take the bus.**

Venderán el perro. **They will sell the dog.**

**Some verbs have a special future stem:**

| | |
|---|---|
| decir (to say) | dir- |
| haber (to have...) | habr- |
| hacer (to do / make) | har- |
| tener (to have) | tendr- |
| poner (to put) | pondr- |

| | |
|---|---|
| querer (to want) | querr- |
| saber (to know) | sabr- |
| venir (to come) | vendr- |
| salir (to go out) | saldr- |
| poder (to be able to) | podr- |

Lo haré mañana. **I will do it tomorrow.**

No vendrá. **She will not come.**

# Would, Could and Should

## The conditional

The conditional can be used to say 'would'. It uses the same stems as the proper future tense.

infinitive / irregular future stem + conditional tense endings

These are the same as the imperfect tense endings for -er and -ir verbs.

| -ar, -er and -ir verbs | |
|---|---|
| -ía | -íamos |
| -ías | -íais |
| -ía | -ían |

Viajaría a Italia.
**I would travel to Italy.**

Viviríamos aquí.
**We would live here.**

Use 'poder' (to be able to) in the conditional to say 'could'.
Use 'deber' (to have to) to say 'should'.

¿Podría ayudarme?
**Could you help me?**

Debería hacer mis deberes.
**I should do my homework.**

Combine the conditional with other tenses to make more complicated sentences.

Bailaría, pero me duelen los pies.
**I would dance, but my feet hurt.**

To say 'would have...', you need the conditional tense of 'haber' (to have...) and a past participle.

Habría comprado un libro, pero no tengo dinero.
**I would have bought a book, but I have no money.**

## 'Quisiera' and 'hubiera'

The conditional form of 'querer' (to want) is often replaced by 'quisiera' to mean 'I would like'. It's often used in polite requests.

'Quisiera' and 'hubiera' are in the imperfect subjunctive.

Quisiera una moto.
**I would like a motorbike.**

Quisiera reservar una mesa para esta noche.
**I would like to reserve a table for tonight.**

The conditional of 'haber' (to have...) can also be replaced by 'hubiera' to mean 'I would have...'.

Hubiera venido antes.
**I would have come earlier.**

# Reflexive Verbs

## Reflexive pronouns

Reflexive verbs are for actions that you do to yourself. They're used with reflexive pronouns, which change depending on who is doing the action.

| | | | |
|---|---|---|---|
| myself | me | ourselves | nos |
| yourself (inf. sing.) | te | yourselves (inf. pl.) | os |
| himself / herself / itself / oneself / yourself (form. sing.) | se | themselves / each other / yourselves (form. pl.) | se |

Reflexive verbs are conjugated just like normal verbs.
The reflexive pronoun usually goes in front of the verb.

| lavarse (to wash oneself) | |
|---|---|
| me **lavo** | nos **lavamos** |
| te **lavas** | os **laváis** |
| se **lava** | se **lavan** |

Me lavo la cara cada mañana.
**I wash my face every morning.**

Se lavan los dientes dos veces al día.
**They brush their teeth twice a day.**

Here are some common reflexive verbs. The verbs on the left are radical-changing.

| | | | |
|---|---|---|---|
| acostarse | *to go to bed* | llamarse | *to be called* |
| despertarse | *to wake up* | levantarse | *to get up* |
| sentirse | *to feel* | irse | *to go away* |
| vestirse | *to get dressed* | ponerse | *to put on* |

Siempre te acuestas muy tarde.
**You always go to bed very late.**

Se despierta a las ocho y media.
**He wakes up at half past eight.**

## Reflexives in the perfect tense

Use reflexive verbs in the perfect tense to say what has happened.
Put the reflexive pronoun in front of the verb as usual.

Me he puesto el sombrero.
**I have put on my hat.**

Se ha acostado.
**She has gone to bed.**

# Verbs with '-ing' and 'Just Done'

## The present continuous

**Use the present continuous to describe something that's happening right now.**

present tense of 'estar' + present participle

The present participle (or gerund) is the '-ing' part.

**Add these endings to the verb stem to form the present participle.**

| -ar verbs | -ando |
|---|---|

| -er and -ir verbs | -iendo |
|---|---|

Estoy almorzando.
**I am having lunch.**

Está poniendo la mesa.
**He is laying the table.**

Están escribiendo.
**They are writing.**

**There are some irregular present participles that you need to know:**

| caer (to fall) | cayendo |
|---|---|
| leer (to read) | leyendo |
| oír (to hear) | oyendo |
| construir (to build) | construyendo |
| ir (to go) | yendo |

| servir (to serve) | sirviendo |
|---|---|
| pedir (to ask for) | pidiendo |
| morir (to die) | muriendo |
| decir (to say) | diciendo |
| dormir (to sleep) | durmiendo |

## The imperfect continuous

**Use the imperfect continuous to say something was happening in the past. It's similar to the present continuous, but 'estar' has to be in the imperfect tense.**

Estaba durmiendo cuando sonó el teléfono.
**She was sleeping when the telephone rang.**

## Acabar de

**To say what's just happened, use the present tense of 'acabar', followed by 'de' and a verb in the infinitive.**

Acabo de ducharme.
**I have just taken a shower.**

# Negative Forms

## Making sentences negative

**To make a sentence negative in any tense, put 'no' in front of the verb.**

Soy profesor. **I'm a teacher.**  No soy profesor. **I'm not a teacher.**

No vas a leer el libro.
**You're not going to read the book.**

No fui al parque.
**I didn't go to the park.**

**'No' means both 'no' and 'not' in Spanish. To answer a question, you may need to say 'no' twice.**

No, no quiero sopa, gracias. **No, I don't want soup, thanks.**

## More negative constructions

| Spanish | English | Example |
|---|---|---|
| ya no | no longer (not anymore) | Ya no voy a Madrid. — I no longer go to Madrid. |
| no ... nadie | nobody (not anybody) | No hay nadie aquí. — There is nobody here. |
| no ... nunca / no ... jamás | never (not ever) | Julia no va nunca al cine. — Julia never goes to the cinema. |
| no ... nada | nothing (not anything) | No hay nada. — There is nothing. |
| no ... ni ... ni | neither ... nor | No van ni a Bath ni a York. — They go to neither Bath nor York. |
| no ... ningún / ninguna | not a single — before noun (none / not one) | No hay ningún plátano. — There isn't a single banana. |
| no ... ninguno/a | not a single one — to replace noun (none / not one) | Chen no tiene ninguno/a. — Chen doesn't have a single one. |

# The Passive and Impersonal Verbs

## The passive voice

In an active sentence, the subject does something.
In the passive voice, something is done to the subject.

Active voice: Lavé la taza. I washed the cup.

Passive voice: La taza fue lavada. The cup was washed.

The passive is formed using 'ser' (to be) and a past participle. The past participle has to agree with the object you're talking about.

Las mesas fueron limpiadas.
The tables were cleaned.

To add someone or something doing the action, add 'por' (by) and who / what does it.

El libro será leído por Jordi. The book will be read by Jordi.

## Impersonal verbs

You can turn any Spanish verb into an impersonal verb (e.g. 'one does') by using the reflexive pronoun 'se' and the third person forms of the verb.

¿Se habla francés aquí?
Does one speak French here?

This can also be translated as 'Is French spoken here?'

Use the 'he/she/it' form for singular subjects...

El arroz se cocina durante quince minutos.
The rice is cooked for fifteen minutes.

...and the 'they' form for plural subjects.

Las puertas se abren a las nueve.
The doors are opened at nine o'clock.

'Hay que' and 'parece que' are common impersonal verbs.

Hay que hacer los deberes.
Homework has to be done.

Parece que todo ha cambiado.
It seems that everything has changed.

Weather verbs are always used in an impersonal way.

Llueve.
It rains.

Está nevando.
It's snowing.

Truena.
It thunders.

'Tronar' (to thunder) is a radical-changing verb.

# The Subjunctive

## Forming the present subjunctive

For '-ar' verbs, add the present tense '-er' endings to the stem of the present tense 'I' form. For '-er' and '-ir' verbs, add the '-ar' endings.

| hablar — 'I' form: hablo | |
|---|---|
| hable | hablemos |
| hables | habléis |
| hable | hablen |

| comer — 'I' form: como | |
|---|---|
| coma | comamos |
| comas | comáis |
| coma | coman |

| vivir — 'I' form: vivo | |
|---|---|
| viva | vivamos |
| vivas | viváis |
| viva | vivan |

Es importante que escuches.
It's important that you listen.

No pienso que coma carne.
I don't think he eats meat.

## Irregular verbs in the present subjunctive

Some verbs are irregular in the 'I' form of the present tense, so the subjunctive has to match this.

| tener (to have) | |
|---|---|
| tenga | tengamos |
| tengas | tengáis |
| tenga | tengan |

| poder (to be able to) | |
|---|---|
| pueda | podamos |
| puedas | podáis |
| pueda | puedan |

The 'we' and 'you (inf. pl.)' forms of radical-changing verbs have regular stems.

Some verbs are completely irregular in the subjunctive:

| | | | | | | |
|---|---|---|---|---|---|---|
| ser (to be) | sea | seas | sea | seamos | seáis | sean |
| estar (to be) | esté | estés | esté | estemos | estéis | estén |
| ir (to go) | vaya | vayas | vaya | vayamos | vayáis | vayan |
| dar (to give) | dé | des | dé | demos | deis | den |
| saber (to know) | sepa | sepas | sepa | sepamos | sepáis | sepan |

# The Subjunctive

## Use the present subjunctive...

1. ...to get someone else to do something.

   Quiero que laves los platos.
   I want you to wash the dishes.

2. ...to express a wish or a desire.

   Espero que haya fresas.
   I hope that there are strawberries.

3. ...after expressing an emotion or opinion.

   Es importante que estudiéis.
   It's important that you study.

4. ...to say that something is unlikely to happen.

   No creo que vaya a visitarnos.
   I don't believe she's going to visit us.

5. ...when there's a requirement.

   Necesito a alguien que sepa cocinar.
   I need someone who knows how to cook.

6. ...after 'antes de que' (before), 'cuando' (when) and 'aunque' (even if) to talk about the future.

   Saldremos cuando lleguen.
   We'll go out when they arrive.

7. ...after 'para que' (so that) to express purpose.

   Salen para que pueda comprar leche.
   They're going out so that he can buy milk.

## The imperfect subjunctive

The imperfect subjunctive is like the 'were' in 'if I were you'.

Si lo describiera, no me creerías.
If I described it, you wouldn't believe me.

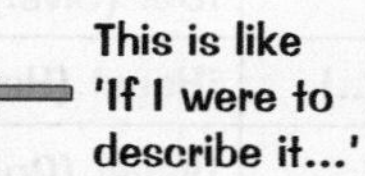

This is like 'If I were to describe it...'

| hablar | |
|---|---|
| hablara | habláramos |
| hablaras | hablarais |
| hablara | hablaran |

| comer | |
|---|---|
| comiera | comiéramos |
| comieras | comierais |
| comiera | comieran |

| vivir | |
|---|---|
| viviera | viviéramos |
| vivieras | vivierais |
| viviera | vivieran |

Era vital que nos escondiéramos.
It was vital that we hid.

Dudo que cantaras mal.
I doubt that you sang badly.

# Giving Orders

## Informal commands

To form a singular informal command, take the 's' off the 'tú' part of the present tense verb.

¡Escribe! Write!

¡Escucha! Listen!

Pronouns go at the end of a command, and you need to add an accent to show where the stress is.

¡Cómelo! Eat it!

For plural informal commands, change the final 'r' of the infinitive to a 'd'.

¡Leed! Read!

¡Salid! Go out!

There are some common irregular informal singular commands:

| | |
|---|---|
| decir (to say) | ¡Di! (Say!) |
| hacer (to do / make) | ¡Haz! (Do! / Make!) |
| ir (to go) | ¡Ve! (Go!) |
| poner (to put) | ¡Pon! (Put!) |

| | |
|---|---|
| salir (to go out) | ¡Sal! (Go out!) |
| ser (to be) | ¡Sé! (Be!) |
| tener (to have) | ¡Ten! (Have!) |
| venir (to come) | ¡Ven! (Come!) |

## Formal commands

For singular formal commands, use the 'usted' form of the present subjunctive. Use the 'ustedes' form for plural formal commands.

¡Hable! Speak!

¡Entren! Enter!

Some common formal commands are irregular:

| | |
|---|---|
| dar (to give) | ¡Dé! (Give!) |
| haber (to have...) | ¡Haya! (Have!) |
| ir (to go) | ¡Vaya! (Go!) |

| | |
|---|---|
| saber (to know) | ¡Sepa! (Know!) |
| ser (to be) | ¡Sea! (Be!) |

## Making commands negative

To tell someone not to do something, always use the present subjunctive.

¡No escuches! Don't listen!

¡No mientas! Don't lie!

Any pronouns have to go before the verb in negative commands.

¡No lo toques! Don't touch it!

¡No las coman! Don't eat them!

SPAN041